LEVEL 3
HOSPITALITY
HOTEL MANAGEMENT

2023

BY CORINA OPREA
SMART-COLLEGE.CO.UK

Hospitality is making your guests feel at home, even when you wish they were.

CONTENT

Module 1: Food Safety and Hygiene

Overview of food safety and hygiene

Understanding food hazards

Food safety legislation and regulations

Personal hygiene and food handling practices

HACCP principles and procedures

Food storage and preservation

Food safety audits and inspections

Module 2: Hospitality and Hotel House Keeping

Introduction to housekeeping

Cleaning methods and techniques

Housekeeping supplies and equipment

Room preparation and servicing

Laundry management

Inventory control and management

Guest satisfaction and complaint handling

Module 3: Customer Service

Understanding customer service in the hospitality industry

Effective communication skills

Meeting and exceeding customer expectations

Handling customer complaints

Managing difficult customers

Building customer loyalty and retention

Service recovery strategies

Module 4: Front Office Operations

Role and responsibilities of front office staff

Front office management and procedures

Reservation systems and procedures

Check-in and check-out procedures

Guest billing and payment methods

Safety and security procedures

Revenue management and sales techniques

Assessment

Module 1: Food Safety and Hygiene

Introduction:

Food safety and hygiene are essential components of the food industry. The safety and hygiene of food refer to the measures that are taken to ensure that food is free from harmful contaminants, pathogens, and other hazardous materials. Food safety and hygiene practices are designed to protect the public from foodborne illnesses and to ensure that food is safe and wholesome for consumption. This essay will discuss the importance of food safety and hygiene, the main causes of food contamination, and the measures that can be taken to ensure food safety and hygiene.

Importance of Food Safety and Hygiene:

Food safety and hygiene are important for several reasons. First, food safety and hygiene practices help prevent foodborne illnesses. These illnesses can be caused by bacteria, viruses, parasites, and other harmful substances that contaminate food. Foodborne illnesses can cause a wide range of symptoms, including nausea, vomiting, diarrhea, and fever. In severe cases, foodborne illnesses can be life-threatening. Therefore, food safety and hygiene practices are essential to prevent the spread of foodborne illnesses.

Second, food safety and hygiene practices help ensure the quality and integrity of food. Food quality is important for both the consumer and the food industry. Consumers want to purchase high-quality food products that are safe and wholesome for consumption. The food industry also benefits from producing high-quality food products, as this can lead to increased sales and customer loyalty.

Third, food safety and hygiene practices are important for regulatory compliance. The food industry is regulated by various government agencies, including the Food and Drug Administration (FDA) and the United States Department of Agriculture (USDA). These agencies have established regulations and guidelines that food producers must follow to ensure the safety and quality of their products. Failure to comply with these regulations can result in fines, legal action, and damage to the reputation of the food producer.

Causes of Food Contamination:

There are several causes of food contamination. These include:

Biological contaminants: These are contaminants that are caused by living organisms such as bacteria, viruses, parasites, and fungi. These organisms can contaminate food during the production, processing, and handling of food products.

Chemical contaminants: These are contaminants that are caused by chemicals such as pesticides, cleaning agents, and food additives. These contaminants can enter the food supply chain during the production, processing, and handling of food products.

Physical contaminants: These are contaminants that are caused by foreign objects such as glass, metal, and plastic. These contaminants can enter the food supply chain during the production, processing, and handling of food products.

Cross-contamination: This is the transfer of harmful contaminants from one food product to another. Cross-contamination can occur during food preparation, cooking, and serving.

Measures to Ensure Food Safety and Hygiene:

There are several measures that can be taken to ensure food safety and hygiene. These include:

Personal hygiene: Personal hygiene is important for anyone who handles food. This includes hand washing, wearing clean clothing and hairnets, and avoiding touching hair, skin, and clothing while handling food.

Cleaning and sanitation: Cleaning and sanitation are important for maintaining a clean and safe food production environment. This includes cleaning and sanitizing all food contact surfaces, equipment, and utensils regularly.

Temperature control: Temperature control is important for preventing the growth of harmful bacteria in food products. This includes maintaining proper storage temperatures for food products, cooking food to the proper internal temperature, and reheating food to the proper temperature.

Hazard Analysis and Critical Control Points (HACCP): HACCP is a systematic approach to identifying and controlling potential hazards in the food production process. This includes identifying potential hazards, establishing critical control points, monitoring these points, and taking corrective action if necessary.

Food labeling: Food labeling is important for ensuring that consumers are aware of any potential allergens or other ingredients that may cause harm. Clear labeling also helps consumers make informed decisions about the food they purchase and consume.

Training and education: Providing training and education to food handlers is important for ensuring that they understand the importance of food safety and hygiene practices. This includes training on personal hygiene, cleaning and sanitation, temperature control, and HACCP.

Regular inspections: Regular inspections by government agencies or third-party auditors are important for ensuring that food producers are complying with regulations and guidelines. Inspections can also identify potential areas for improvement and help prevent foodborne illnesses.

Conclusion:

Food safety and hygiene are essential components of the food industry. Food producers must take measures to ensure that their products are safe and wholesome for consumption. Failure to do so can result in serious health consequences for consumers and damage to the reputation of the food producer. By implementing personal hygiene practices, cleaning and sanitation procedures, temperature control measures, HACCP, food labeling, training and education, and regular inspections, food producers can help prevent foodborne illnesses and ensure the quality and integrity of their products.

Food safety and hygiene refer to the measures taken to ensure that food is free from harmful contaminants, pathogens, and other hazardous materials. It is essential to ensure the safety and hygiene of food, as foodborne illnesses can have serious health consequences for consumers. This essay will provide an overview of food safety and hygiene, including the main causes of food contamination, the importance of food safety and hygiene, and the measures that can be taken to ensure food safety and hygiene.

Causes of Food Contamination:

There are several causes of food contamination. These include:

Biological contaminants: These are contaminants that are caused by living organisms such as bacteria, viruses, parasites, and fungi. These organisms can contaminate food during the production, processing, and handling of food products. For example, Salmonella and E. coli are common bacteria that can cause foodborne illnesses if they contaminate food products.

Chemical contaminants: These are contaminants that are caused by chemicals such as pesticides, cleaning agents, and food additives. These contaminants can enter the food supply chain during the production, processing, and handling of food products. For example, pesticides used to protect crops can contaminate food products if not used properly.

Physical contaminants: These are contaminants that are caused by foreign objects such as glass, metal, and plastic. These contaminants can enter the food supply chain during the production, processing, and handling of food products. For example, a broken piece of glass from a light bulb can fall into food products during processing.

Cross-contamination: This is the transfer of harmful contaminants from one food product to another. Cross-contamination can occur during food preparation, cooking, and serving. For example, if a cutting board is used to prepare raw meat and is not cleaned properly before being used to prepare vegetables, the vegetables can become contaminated with harmful bacteria.

Importance of Food Safety and Hygiene:

Food safety and hygiene are important for several reasons. First, food safety and hygiene practices help prevent foodborne illnesses. These illnesses can be caused by bacteria, viruses, parasites, and other harmful substances that contaminate food. Foodborne illnesses can cause a wide range of symptoms, including nausea, vomiting, diarrhea, and fever. In severe cases, foodborne illnesses can be life-threatening. Therefore, food safety and hygiene practices are essential to prevent the spread of foodborne illnesses.

Second, food safety and hygiene practices help ensure the quality and integrity of food. Food quality is important for both the consumer and the food industry. Consumers want to purchase high-quality food products that are safe and wholesome for consumption. The food industry also benefits from producing high-quality food products, as this can lead to increased sales and customer loyalty.

Third, food safety and hygiene practices are important for regulatory compliance. The food industry is regulated by various government agencies, including the Food and Drug Administration (FDA) and the United States Department of Agriculture (USDA). These agencies have established regulations and guidelines that food producers must follow to ensure the safety and quality of their products. Failure to comply with these regulations can result in fines, legal action, and damage to the reputation of the food producer.

Measures to Ensure Food Safety and Hygiene:

There are several measures that can be taken to ensure food safety and hygiene. These include:

Personal hygiene: Personal hygiene is important for anyone who handles food. This includes hand washing, wearing clean clothing and hairnets, and avoiding touching hair, skin, and clothing while handling food.

Cleaning and sanitation: Cleaning and sanitation are important for maintaining a clean and safe food production environment. This includes cleaning and sanitizing all food contact surfaces, equipment, and utensils regularly.

Temperature control: Temperature control is important for preventing the growth of harmful bacteria in food products. This includes keeping hot foods hot and cold foods cold during storage and transportation. Food must be cooked to the appropriate temperature to ensure that harmful bacteria are killed.

HACCP (Hazard Analysis and Critical Control Points): HACCP is a food safety management system that focuses on identifying and controlling potential hazards in the food production process. HACCP identifies critical control points where hazards can be controlled, and monitoring procedures are put in place to ensure that these control points are functioning properly.

Food labeling: Food labeling is important for ensuring that consumers are aware of any potential allergens or other ingredients that may cause harm. Clear labeling also helps consumers make informed decisions about the food they purchase and consume.

Training and education: Providing training and education to food handlers is important for ensuring that they understand the importance of food safety and hygiene practices. This includes training on personal hygiene, cleaning and sanitation, temperature control, and HACCP.

Regular inspections: Regular inspections by government agencies or third-party auditors are important for ensuring that food producers are complying with regulations and guidelines. Inspections can also identify potential areas for improvement and help prevent foodborne illnesses.

Conclusion:

In conclusion, food safety and hygiene are critical aspects of the food industry. Food producers must take measures to ensure that their products are safe and wholesome for consumption. Failure to do so can result in serious health consequences for consumers and damage to the reputation of the food producer. By implementing personal hygiene practices, cleaning and sanitation procedures, temperature control measures, HACCP, food labeling, training and education, and regular inspections, food producers can help prevent foodborne illnesses and ensure the quality and integrity of their products.

Food hazards are any biological, chemical, or physical agent that can cause harm to consumers when they are present in food. Understanding food hazards is critical to ensure the safety and quality of food products. This essay will provide an overview of the different types of food hazards, their sources, and the measures that can be taken to prevent their occurrence.

Types of Food Hazards:

There are three main types of food hazards:

Biological hazards: These are hazards that are caused by living organisms such as bacteria, viruses, parasites, and fungi. Biological hazards can cause foodborne illnesses, which can range from mild symptoms such as nausea and diarrhea to severe illnesses such as kidney failure and death. Examples of common biological hazards include Salmonella, E. coli, Listeria, and Campylobacter.

Chemical hazards: These are hazards that are caused by chemicals such as pesticides, cleaning agents, food additives, and natural toxins. Chemical hazards can cause acute or chronic health effects depending on the type and level of exposure. Examples of common chemical hazards include heavy metals such as lead and mercury, mycotoxins produced by molds, and food dyes.

Physical hazards: These are hazards that are caused by foreign objects such as glass, metal, plastic, and bone fragments. Physical hazards can cause injury to the consumer, such as choking or lacerations. Examples of common physical hazards include broken glass from light bulbs, metal shavings from equipment, and bone fragments in meat products.

Sources of Food Hazards:

Food hazards can originate from different sources, including:

Raw materials: Food hazards can be present in raw materials such as fruits, vegetables, and meat products. These hazards can result from the use of contaminated water or soil, poor animal husbandry practices, or improper handling during transportation and storage.

Processing: Food hazards can also result from processing operations such as cutting, grinding, and packaging. Cross-contamination can occur when equipment is not cleaned properly between different production runs, and microbial growth can occur when food is not stored at the appropriate temperature.

Storage and transportation: Food hazards can also result from improper storage and transportation conditions. For example, food can become contaminated during storage if it is stored at the wrong temperature or if it is stored near chemicals or other contaminants.

Prevention of Food Hazards:

Preventing food hazards is critical to ensure the safety and quality of food products. There are several measures that can be taken to prevent the occurrence of food hazards, including:

Good manufacturing practices: Good manufacturing practices (GMPs) are a set of guidelines that outline the minimum requirements for food safety and quality. GMPs cover areas such as personal hygiene, equipment maintenance and cleaning, pest control, and product handling.

Hazard Analysis and Critical Control Points (HACCP): HACCP is a systematic approach to identifying and controlling hazards throughout the food production process. HACCP involves identifying potential hazards, setting up monitoring procedures, and taking corrective actions if necessary.

Quality control: Quality control involves monitoring and testing food products to ensure that they meet specific quality and safety standards. Quality control measures can include physical and chemical testing, sensory evaluation, and microbiological analysis.

Proper storage and transportation: Proper storage and transportation are critical to preventing food hazards. This includes ensuring that food is stored at the appropriate temperature and that it is transported in clean and properly maintained vehicles.

Education and training: Education and training are essential to ensuring that food handlers understand the importance of food safety and hygiene practices. This includes training on personal hygiene, cleaning and sanitation, temperature control, and HACCP.

Regular inspections: Regular inspections by government agencies or third-party auditors are important for ensuring that food producers are complying with regulations and guidelines

and that their products are safe and of high quality. Inspections can also identify potential areas for improvement and help prevent foodborne illnesses.

Traceability: Traceability refers to the ability to track a food product from the farm or source of origin to the consumer. Traceability systems can help identify the source of a foodborne illness outbreak and allow for quick recall of contaminated products.

Conclusion:

In conclusion, understanding food hazards is critical to ensure the safety and quality of food products. Biological, chemical, and physical hazards can all pose a risk to consumers if they are present in food. These hazards can originate from different sources, including raw materials, processing operations, and storage and transportation conditions. Preventing food hazards requires a combination of good manufacturing practices, HACCP, quality control, proper storage and transportation, education and training, regular inspections, and traceability. By implementing these measures, food producers can help prevent foodborne illnesses and ensure that their products are safe and of high quality.

Food safety legislation and regulations are a set of rules and guidelines designed to ensure the safety and quality of food products. These regulations are put in place to protect consumers from the risks associated with consuming contaminated or unsafe food. This essay will provide an overview of the different types of food safety legislation and regulations, their purpose, and how they are enforced.

Types of Food Safety Legislation and Regulations:

Food Safety Modernization Act (FSMA): The FSMA was signed into law in 2011 and is the most significant food safety legislation in the United States in over 70 years. The FSMA aims to prevent foodborne illnesses by shifting the focus from responding to outbreaks to preventing them from occurring in the first place. The FSMA includes several key provisions, including mandatory preventive controls for food facilities, a new inspection regime for imported foods, and a requirement for food companies to have a written food safety plan.

Food and Drug Administration (FDA) Food Code: The FDA Food Code is a model food safety code that provides guidance to food service establishments, retail food stores, and food vending operations on how to prevent foodborne illnesses. The code covers topics such as food storage and preparation, employee hygiene, and equipment maintenance.

Hazard Analysis and Critical Control Points (HACCP): HACCP is a systematic approach to identifying and controlling food safety hazards throughout the food production process. HACCP is a mandatory requirement for certain types of food establishments, such as meat and poultry processing facilities.

Codex Alimentarius: Codex Alimentarius is a collection of internationally recognized food safety standards and guidelines developed by the Food and Agriculture Organization (FAO) and the World Health Organization (WHO). The Codex Alimentarius covers a wide range of topics, including food labeling, food additives, and food contaminants.

Purpose of Food Safety Legislation and Regulations:

The purpose of food safety legislation and regulations is to protect consumers from the risks associated with consuming contaminated or unsafe food. Foodborne illnesses can result in severe health consequences and even death, making food safety a critical issue. Food safety regulations aim to prevent foodborne illnesses by establishing standards for the production, processing, and handling of food products.

In addition to protecting consumers, food safety regulations also help to maintain public confidence in the food supply. When consumers trust that the food they are consuming is safe and of high quality, they are more likely to purchase and consume food products. This, in turn, benefits the food industry by maintaining demand for their products.

Enforcement of Food Safety Legislation and Regulations:

Food safety legislation and regulations are enforced by government agencies and regulatory bodies. In the United States, the FDA is responsible for regulating the safety of most food products. The USDA is responsible for regulating the safety of meat, poultry, and egg products. State and local health departments also play a role in enforcing food safety regulations.

Enforcement of food safety regulations typically involves inspections of food facilities to ensure that they are complying with regulations and guidelines. Inspectors may review records, check equipment, and observe food handling and preparation practices. If violations are found, the facility may be required to take corrective action, such as implementing new procedures or recalling products.

Penalties for violating food safety regulations can range from fines to criminal charges. In severe cases, facilities may be forced to close, and individuals may face imprisonment.

Challenges in Food Safety Regulation:

Despite the importance of food safety regulation, there are several challenges in enforcing these regulations. One challenge is the global nature of the food supply chain. As food products are increasingly sourced from around the world, it can be difficult to ensure that all producers are following the same standards and regulations.

Another challenge is the limited resources available for inspections and enforcement. Government agencies are often stretched thin, and there may not be enough resources to conduct regular inspections of all food facilities. This can make it challenging to identify and prevent potential hazards before they lead to a foodborne illness outbreak.

Additionally, the constantly evolving nature of the food industry can make it difficult to keep regulations up-to-date. New technologies, processing methods, and ingredients may require updates to existing regulations or the creation of new regulations.

Finally, compliance with food safety regulations is not always a guarantee of safety. Despite following all regulations and guidelines, food facilities can still experience outbreaks of foodborne illnesses. This highlights the need for ongoing research and development in the area of food safety.

Conclusion:

Food safety legislation and regulations play a critical role in ensuring the safety and quality of food products. These regulations are designed to protect consumers from the risks associated with consuming contaminated or unsafe food. They also help to maintain public confidence in the food supply, which benefits the food industry as a whole.

Enforcement of food safety regulations involves inspections of food facilities and penalties for violations. However, there are several challenges in enforcing these regulations, including the global nature of the food supply chain, limited resources for inspections and enforcement, and the constantly evolving nature of the food industry.

Despite these challenges, food safety regulations are an essential component of protecting public health. Ongoing research and development in the area of food safety are needed to ensure that regulations keep pace with new technologies, processing methods, and ingredients, and that the food supply remains safe and of high quality.

Personal hygiene and food handling practices are critical factors in preventing foodborne illnesses. Good personal hygiene practices among food handlers are essential to ensuring that the food they prepare and serve is safe for consumption. This includes maintaining proper handwashing techniques, wearing appropriate clothing and personal protective equipment, and avoiding behaviors that can contaminate food. In this article, we will explore the importance of personal hygiene and food handling practices in preventing foodborne illnesses.

Handwashing:

One of the most important personal hygiene practices for food handlers is proper handwashing. Hands are a major source of contamination in the food handling process, and it is essential that food handlers wash their hands thoroughly and frequently throughout the day. Proper handwashing involves wetting the hands with warm water, applying soap, lathering the hands for at least 20 seconds, rinsing the hands thoroughly, and drying them with a clean towel or air dryer. Handwashing should be done before handling food, after using the restroom, after handling garbage or cleaning supplies, and after touching any part of the body or clothing.

Clothing and Personal Protective Equipment:

Food handlers should wear appropriate clothing and personal protective equipment (PPE) to prevent contamination of food. This includes wearing clean uniforms or aprons, hair restraints, and gloves. Clothing should be made of materials that are easy to clean and sanitize, and gloves should be changed frequently to prevent cross-contamination. Hair restraints should be worn to prevent hair from falling into food, and jewelry should be kept to a minimum to prevent it from falling into food.

Avoiding Behaviors That Can Contaminate Food:

Food handlers should avoid behaviors that can contaminate food, such as smoking, chewing gum, or eating while preparing or serving food. They should also avoid touching their face, hair, or any other part of their body while handling food. Additionally, food handlers should not work while they are sick, as they can easily transmit illness to the food they handle.

Temperature Control:

Proper temperature control is essential to preventing the growth of bacteria that can cause foodborne illnesses. Food should be stored at the appropriate temperature to prevent bacterial growth, and food handlers should monitor the temperature of food and equipment regularly. Additionally, food should be cooked to the appropriate temperature to kill any bacteria that may be present.

Cleaning and Sanitizing:

Proper cleaning and sanitizing of equipment and surfaces is critical to preventing the spread of bacteria in food facilities. Food handlers should follow established cleaning and sanitizing procedures, which typically involve washing with soap and water, rinsing, and then applying a sanitizing solution.

Equipment and surfaces that come into contact with food should be sanitized frequently throughout the day.

Food Storage:

Proper food storage is essential to preventing contamination of food. Food should be stored in designated areas, away from chemicals and other potentially hazardous materials. Raw meat and poultry should be stored separately from other foods to prevent cross-contamination, and food should be stored at the appropriate temperature to prevent bacterial growth.

Conclusion:

Personal hygiene and food handling practices are critical factors in preventing foodborne illnesses. Food handlers must maintain proper handwashing techniques, wear appropriate clothing and personal protective equipment, and avoid behaviors that can contaminate food. Additionally, they must ensure proper temperature control, cleaning and sanitizing, and food storage to prevent the spread of bacteria. Adhering to these practices can help ensure that the food served to customers is safe and of high quality.

Hazard Analysis and Critical Control Points (HACCP) is a system that was developed to ensure the safety of food products. HACCP principles and procedures are used to identify potential hazards in the food production process, and to establish control measures to prevent these hazards from occurring. In this article, we will explore the principles and procedures of HACCP and how they are applied in the food industry.

HACCP Principles:

The HACCP system is based on seven principles, which are as follows:

Conduct a Hazard Analysis: The first step in implementing HACCP is to conduct a hazard analysis. This involves identifying potential hazards that could occur at each stage of the food production process, from raw material procurement to final product delivery.

Determine Critical Control Points (CCPs): CCPs are points in the production process where control measures can be implemented to prevent or eliminate a hazard. These are typically identified during the hazard analysis process.

Establish Critical Limits: Critical limits are the maximum or minimum values that must be met at each CCP to ensure that the hazard is controlled. These are based on scientific data and may include time and temperature parameters, pH levels, or other factors.

Establish Monitoring Procedures: Monitoring procedures are put in place to ensure that the critical limits are being met at each CCP. This may involve visual inspections, temperature readings, or other methods of measurement.

Establish Corrective Actions: If a critical limit is not met at a CCP, corrective actions must be taken to bring the process back under control. These actions may include adjusting process parameters, reworking product, or stopping production altogether.

Establish Verification Procedures: Verification procedures are put in place to ensure that the HACCP system is working effectively. This may involve testing samples of product, reviewing records, or conducting audits.

Establish Record-Keeping and Documentation Procedures: Accurate record-keeping is essential to the HACCP system. All procedures, processes, and activities related to food production must be documented and retained for a specific period of time.

Application of HACCP Principles:

HACCP principles are used in the food industry to ensure the safety and quality of food products. This includes the following applications:

Raw Material Procurement: HACCP principles are used to ensure that raw materials used in the production of food products are safe and of high quality.

Production Process: HACCP principles are used to identify potential hazards in the production process and to establish control measures to prevent these hazards from occurring. This may involve controlling temperature, pH levels, or other factors that can impact the safety of the food product.

Packaging and Storage: HACCP principles are used to ensure that food products are packaged and stored in a safe and appropriate manner. This may involve controlling temperature and humidity levels, ensuring that packaging materials are safe, and implementing appropriate storage procedures.

Transportation and Delivery: HACCP principles are used to ensure that food products are transported and delivered in a safe and timely manner. This may involve implementing appropriate transportation and delivery procedures, monitoring temperature and other conditions during transportation, and ensuring that the delivery vehicle is clean and well-maintained.

Benefits of HACCP:

The HACCP system offers several benefits to the food industry, including:

Improved Food Safety: By identifying and controlling potential hazards in the food production process, the HACCP system helps to improve the safety of food products.

Increased Quality: The HACCP system can help to improve the overall quality of food products by ensuring that they are produced in a consistent and controlled manner.

Compliance with Regulations: The HACCP system is required by many food safety regulations and can help food manufacturers to comply with these regulations.

Reduced Costs: By identifying potential hazards and implementing control measures, the HACCP system can help to reduce the risk of product recalls and other costly issues.

Conclusion:

HACCP principles and procedures are essential to ensuring the safety and quality of food products. By identifying potential hazards and implementing control measures, the HACCP system helps to reduce the risk of foodborne illness and other food safety issues. The HACCP system is required by many food safety regulations and can help food manufacturers to comply with these regulations. Overall, the HACCP system offers numerous benefits to the food industry and plays a critical role in ensuring the safety and quality of food products.

Food safety audits and inspections are important tools for ensuring the safety and quality of the food supply chain. Audits and inspections help to identify potential hazards and risks within the food supply chain, and help to ensure that food products are produced, stored, and distributed in accordance with established food safety standards and regulations. In this article, we will discuss the importance of food safety audits and inspections, as well as the types of audits and inspections that are commonly used in the food industry.

Importance of Food Safety Audits and Inspections:

Food safety audits and inspections are important for several reasons:

Compliance with Regulations: Audits and inspections help to ensure that food products are produced, stored, and distributed in accordance with established food safety regulations.

Risk Assessment: Audits and inspections help to identify potential hazards and risks within the food supply chain.

Quality Assurance: Audits and inspections help to ensure that food products are of a consistent quality, and meet customer expectations.

Brand Protection: Audits and inspections help to protect a company's brand by ensuring that their products are safe and of a high quality.

Types of Food Safety Audits and Inspections:

There are several types of food safety audits and inspections that are commonly used in the food industry, including:

Internal Audits: Internal audits are conducted by a company's own staff to assess compliance with internal policies and procedures.

Third-Party Audits: Third-party audits are conducted by an independent organization to assess compliance with external standards and regulations.

Regulatory Inspections: Regulatory inspections are conducted by government agencies to assess compliance with food safety regulations.

Supplier Audits: Supplier audits are conducted to assess the quality and safety of products and services provided by suppliers.

GMP Audits: Good Manufacturing Practice (GMP) audits are conducted to assess compliance with established manufacturing standards.

HACCP Audits: Hazard Analysis and Critical Control Point (HACCP) audits are conducted to assess compliance with established food safety management systems.

Process of Food Safety Audits and Inspections:

The process of food safety audits and inspections typically involves several steps, including:

Preparation: Preparation involves gathering information about the facility or process being audited or inspected, such as documentation, standard operating procedures, and previous audit reports.

On-Site Inspection: The on-site inspection involves conducting a physical assessment of the facility or process being audited or inspected, including observation of operations, testing of equipment and processes, and review of documentation.

Reporting: After the on-site inspection, a report is generated that summarizes the findings of the audit or inspection, and provides recommendations for corrective actions if necessary.

Follow-up: Follow-up involves ensuring that corrective actions are taken in response to any findings or recommendations identified in the audit or inspection report.

Conclusion:

Food safety audits and inspections are important tools for ensuring the safety and quality of the food supply chain. Audits and inspections help to identify potential hazards and risks within the food supply chain, and help to ensure that food products are produced, stored, and distributed in accordance with established food safety standards and regulations. There are several types of food safety audits and inspections that are commonly used in the food industry, including internal audits, third-party audits, regulatory inspections, supplier audits, GMP audits, and HACCP audits. The process of food safety audits and inspections typically involves several steps, including preparation, on-site inspection, reporting, and follow-up. By implementing a robust food safety audit and inspection program, companies can help to ensure the safety and quality of their food products, protect their brand, and comply with regulatory requirements.

Module 2: Hospitality and Hotel House Keeping

Hospitality and hotel housekeeping are essential components of the hotel industry. The housekeeping department of a hotel is responsible for ensuring that the hotel is clean and presentable for guests. The hospitality industry is centered around providing a positive experience for guests, and housekeeping plays a crucial role in making that experience a reality. In this article, we will discuss the importance of hospitality and hotel housekeeping, as well as the responsibilities of housekeeping staff.

Importance of Hospitality and Hotel Housekeeping:

The importance of hospitality and hotel housekeeping can be summarized as follows:

First Impressions: The cleanliness and overall appearance of a hotel can leave a lasting impression on guests. A well-maintained hotel with a clean and comfortable environment can create a positive impression on guests, which can lead to repeat business and positive word-of-mouth.

Guest Satisfaction: A clean and comfortable environment can contribute to guest satisfaction. Happy guests are more likely to return to a hotel and recommend it to others.

Health and Safety: Maintaining a clean and safe environment is essential for the health and safety of guests and staff. A clean environment reduces the risk of accidents and illnesses.

Responsibilities of Housekeeping Staff:

The housekeeping department of a hotel is responsible for a range of duties, including:

Room Cleaning: The primary responsibility of housekeeping staff is to clean and maintain guest rooms. This involves changing linens, cleaning bathrooms, vacuuming carpets, and dusting surfaces.

Public Area Cleaning: Housekeeping staff is also responsible for cleaning public areas of the hotel, such as hallways, lobbies, and elevators.

Laundry Services: Housekeeping staff is responsible for laundering hotel linens and towels, as well as guest laundry if the hotel provides this service.

Inventory Management: Housekeeping staff is responsible for managing inventory of cleaning supplies and linens.

Guest Services: Housekeeping staff may also assist guests with requests such as providing extra towels, pillows, or blankets.

Challenges Faced by Housekeeping Staff:

Housekeeping staff face a range of challenges in their daily work, including:

Time Constraints: Housekeeping staff is often under pressure to clean rooms quickly, which can lead to shortcuts that compromise the quality of the cleaning.

Language Barriers: Housekeeping staff may have difficulty communicating with guests who speak different languages.

Physical Demands: Housekeeping work can be physically demanding, as staff may need to lift heavy objects and stand for extended periods.

Repetitive Tasks: Housekeeping staff may experience repetitive stress injuries due to the repetitive nature of their work.

Staffing Issues: Housekeeping departments may struggle to recruit and retain staff, which can lead to increased workloads for existing staff.

Strategies for Improving Hospitality and Hotel Housekeeping:

To improve hospitality and hotel housekeeping, several strategies can be implemented, including:

Training: Providing comprehensive training for housekeeping staff on cleaning techniques, safety procedures, and guest service can improve the quality of their work and enhance guest satisfaction.

Communication: Improving communication between housekeeping staff and guests can help to address concerns and improve the guest experience.

Equipment and Supplies: Providing high-quality cleaning equipment and supplies can improve the efficiency and effectiveness of housekeeping staff.

Ergonomic Design: Implementing ergonomic design principles in hotel rooms and public spaces can reduce the physical demands of housekeeping work.

Staffing and Scheduling: Ensuring that housekeeping departments are adequately staffed and providing reasonable workloads can reduce staff turnover and improve the quality of work.

Conclusion:

Hospitality and hotel housekeeping are essential components of the hotel industry. The cleanliness and overall appearance of a hotel can leave a lasting impression on guests, and a well-maintained hotel can contribute to guest satisfaction and safety. The responsibilities of housekeeping staff include room cleaning, public area cleaning, laundry services, inventory management, and guest services. However, housekeeping staff face several challenges, including time constraints, language barriers, physical demands, repetitive tasks, and staffing issues.

To improve hospitality and hotel housekeeping, training, communication, equipment and supplies, ergonomic design, staffing and scheduling strategies can be implemented. Providing comprehensive training for housekeeping staff, improving communication between staff and guests, providing high-quality cleaning equipment and supplies, implementing ergonomic design principles, and ensuring that departments are adequately staffed and scheduled can improve the quality of work and enhance guest satisfaction.

In conclusion, hospitality and hotel housekeeping are crucial aspects of the hotel industry. The cleanliness and overall appearance of a hotel can leave a lasting impression on guests, and a well-maintained hotel can contribute to guest satisfaction and safety. Housekeeping staff play a vital role in ensuring that hotels are clean and presentable for guests. Implementing strategies to improve hospitality and hotel housekeeping can enhance the guest experience and contribute to the success of the hotel industry.

Housekeeping is the department responsible for ensuring that a facility, such as a hotel, resort, or hospital, is clean, safe, and well-maintained. The housekeeping department is critical to the success of any facility, as it contributes to the overall guest experience and safety.

In a hotel setting, the housekeeping department is responsible for cleaning and maintaining guest rooms, public areas, and laundry services. The department is also responsible for managing inventory, responding to guest requests, and ensuring that the hotel is compliant with health and safety regulations.

Housekeeping staff typically work in shifts and perform a variety of tasks, such as making beds, cleaning bathrooms, dusting and vacuuming, restocking amenities, and managing laundry services. The department also works closely with other departments, such as maintenance and front desk, to ensure that guest needs are met promptly.

The role of housekeeping in the hotel industry is critical. A well-maintained hotel is essential for guest comfort, safety, and satisfaction. Therefore, housekeeping staff must be well-trained, efficient, and detail-oriented. They must also be able to work independently and as part of a team to meet the needs of guests.

Housekeeping staff must have a comprehensive understanding of cleaning chemicals and equipment to ensure that they can effectively clean and maintain the hotel. They must also be familiar with health and safety regulations and the proper use of personal protective equipment to protect themselves and guests from harm.

Overall, the housekeeping department is essential to the success of any facility in the hospitality industry. The department's ability to maintain cleanliness, safety, and overall appearance can contribute to guest satisfaction and safety. Therefore, it is critical that housekeeping staff are well-trained, efficient, and equipped with the necessary tools and resources to perform their duties effectively.

Effective cleaning methods and techniques are crucial for maintaining a clean and healthy environment. Whether in a commercial or residential setting, it is essential to employ the right cleaning methods and techniques to remove dirt, dust, and harmful pathogens effectively. The following are some of the most common cleaning methods and techniques:

Dry Cleaning: Dry cleaning involves using absorbent materials or machines that do not use water to clean surfaces. Dry cleaning is suitable for removing dry dust and soil from carpets, upholstery, and other delicate surfaces. Some common dry cleaning techniques include vacuuming, brushing, and using dry cleaning solvents.

Wet Cleaning: Wet cleaning involves using water and cleaning solutions to remove dirt and stains from surfaces. Wet cleaning is ideal for floors, walls, and surfaces that can withstand water. The most common wet cleaning techniques include mopping, scrubbing, and pressure washing.

Steam Cleaning: Steam cleaning is a method that uses high-temperature steam to clean and disinfect surfaces. Steam cleaning is effective in killing bacteria and viruses and is ideal for surfaces that require deep cleaning, such as carpets and upholstery.

Chemical Cleaning: Chemical cleaning involves using cleaning solutions to break down and remove dirt and stains from surfaces. Chemical cleaning is ideal for removing grease, oil, and other tough stains. However, chemical cleaning can be harmful to the environment and may require personal protective equipment.

Ultrasonic Cleaning: Ultrasonic cleaning uses high-frequency sound waves to remove dirt and stains from surfaces. Ultrasonic cleaning is ideal for delicate surfaces and can be used to clean jewelry, eyeglasses, and other small items.

In addition to the cleaning methods, there are several techniques that can be used to ensure effective cleaning. These techniques include:

Surface Preparation: Surface preparation involves removing loose debris and clutter from surfaces before cleaning. This technique helps to ensure that the cleaning solution can penetrate the surface and remove dirt and stains effectively.

Agitation: Agitation involves using a brush or other tool to scrub the surface and remove dirt and stains. Agitation helps to break down and remove stubborn stains and is often used in conjunction with cleaning solutions.

Dwell Time: Dwell time is the amount of time that a cleaning solution is allowed to sit on a surface before being rinsed or wiped away. Dwell time allows the cleaning solution to penetrate the surface and remove dirt and stains effectively.

Rinsing: Rinsing involves using water to remove cleaning solutions and dirt from surfaces. Rinsing is essential to prevent the buildup of cleaning solutions and to ensure that surfaces are clean and free of residue.

Drying: Drying involves removing excess moisture from surfaces after cleaning. Drying helps to prevent the growth of mold and bacteria and ensures that surfaces are clean and safe.

In conclusion, effective cleaning methods and techniques are essential for maintaining a clean and healthy environment. Dry cleaning, wet cleaning, steam cleaning, chemical cleaning, and ultrasonic cleaning are some of the most common cleaning methods. Surface preparation, agitation, dwell time, rinsing, and drying are some of the most common cleaning techniques. By employing the right cleaning methods and techniques, it is possible to maintain a clean and healthy environment and prevent the spread of harmful pathogens.

Room preparation and servicing are crucial aspects of housekeeping in the hospitality industry. It is the responsibility of the housekeeping staff to ensure that guest rooms are clean, comfortable, and welcoming. The following are some of the key tasks involved in room preparation and servicing:

Room Inspection: Before preparing a room for a guest, housekeeping staff should inspect the room to ensure that it is clean and ready for occupancy. This includes checking the bedding, towels, and amenities, as well as ensuring that the room is free of dust and debris.

Bed Making: One of the primary tasks of room preparation and servicing is making the bed. The bed should be made with fresh, clean linens and should be properly arranged to create a comfortable and inviting environment for the guest.

Cleaning and Sanitizing: Housekeeping staff should thoroughly clean and sanitize all surfaces in the room, including floors, walls, furniture, and fixtures. This includes using appropriate cleaning solutions and disinfectants to ensure that the room is free of harmful pathogens.

Restocking Amenities: Housekeeping staff should ensure that all amenities are fully stocked, including towels, toiletries, and other guest supplies. This includes checking the inventory of items and restocking as needed to ensure that guests have everything they need for a comfortable stay.

Trash and Recycling: Housekeeping staff should empty all trash and recycling bins in the room and ensure that they are properly disposed of. This includes separating recyclable materials and disposing of hazardous waste in a safe and responsible manner.

Room Maintenance: Housekeeping staff should also perform routine maintenance tasks in the room, such as checking light bulbs, replacing batteries in remote controls, and addressing any issues with the HVAC system or other equipment.

Guest Requests: Housekeeping staff should respond promptly to guest requests, such as providing additional pillows or blankets, providing extra towels or toiletries, or addressing any maintenance issues in the room.

Departure Cleaning: When a guest checks out of a room, housekeeping staff should perform a thorough cleaning and sanitizing of the room, including changing the bedding, cleaning all surfaces, and restocking amenities for the next guest.

In addition to these tasks, there are several best practices that housekeeping staff can follow to ensure that they provide the highest level of service to guests. These best practices include:

Attention to Detail: Housekeeping staff should pay close attention to detail and ensure that every aspect of the room is clean and well-maintained. This includes checking for stains, dust, and other signs of wear and tear.

Professionalism: Housekeeping staff should maintain a professional demeanor at all times and interact with guests in a courteous and respectful manner. This includes being attentive to guest requests and ensuring that all interactions are handled with care.

Time Management: Housekeeping staff should manage their time effectively and prioritize tasks to ensure that they can complete all tasks within the allotted time frame. This includes being proactive and anticipating guest needs to ensure that they are met in a timely manner.

Communication: Housekeeping staff should communicate effectively with other members of the hotel staff, including front desk personnel, maintenance staff, and management. This includes reporting any issues or concerns promptly and providing updates on room status and guest requests.

In conclusion, room preparation and servicing are critical aspects of housekeeping in the hospitality industry. Housekeeping staff should be attentive to detail, professional, and efficient in their work, and should prioritize the needs of guests to ensure that they have a comfortable and enjoyable stay. By following best practices and taking a proactive approach to their work, housekeeping staff can provide a high level of service and contribute to the overall success of the hotel.

Laundry management is an essential component of housekeeping in the hospitality industry. It involves the management of laundry services for both guests and staff, including the laundering of linens, towels, and other textiles used in hotel operations. Proper laundry management is critical to ensuring that guests have a comfortable and hygienic experience during their stay, and that staff have access to clean uniforms and work clothing. The following are some key elements of laundry management in the hospitality industry:

Equipment and Facilities: The first step in laundry management is to ensure that the hotel has the proper equipment and facilities to handle laundry operations. This includes commercial-grade washing machines, dryers, and ironing equipment, as well as adequate space for storing and organizing laundry.

Inventory Management: Proper inventory management is critical to ensuring that there are enough linens and towels to meet guest needs, without overstocking and wasting resources. This includes tracking inventory levels, monitoring usage rates, and forecasting demand to ensure that the hotel has an adequate supply of clean linens and towels at all times.

Laundry Procedures: The actual laundering process involves several steps, including sorting, washing, drying, and folding. Housekeeping staff should follow established procedures for each of these steps to ensure that laundry is cleaned properly and efficiently. This includes separating linens by color and fabric type, using appropriate detergents and other cleaning agents, and ensuring that all laundry is properly dried and folded.

Quality Control: Quality control is critical in laundry management to ensure that linens and towels are cleaned to the highest standards. This includes conducting regular quality control checks to ensure that laundry is free of stains, odors, and other signs of wear and tear, as well as ensuring that linens are properly ironed and folded.

Staff Training: Housekeeping staff should be trained in proper laundry management procedures to ensure that they can perform their duties effectively and efficiently. This includes training on proper laundry procedures, equipment operation, and quality control, as well as safety protocols and hazard communication.

Sustainability: Sustainable laundry management is an increasingly important issue in the hospitality industry, as hotels seek to reduce their environmental impact and conserve resources. This includes implementing energy-efficient laundry equipment, using eco-friendly cleaning products, and reducing water and energy usage during the laundering process.

Outsourcing: Some hotels may choose to outsource laundry management to third-party vendors, which can provide specialized expertise and equipment. This can be especially useful for smaller hotels or hotels with limited laundry facilities.

Effective laundry management is critical to ensuring that guests have a comfortable and hygienic experience during their stay, and that staff have access to clean uniforms and work clothing. By implementing best practices and investing in the proper equipment and training, hotels can ensure that their laundry operations run smoothly and efficiently, while also minimizing their environmental impact and reducing waste.

Inventory control and management is a critical aspect of running a successful business, regardless of the industry. It involves the systematic tracking, monitoring, and optimization of inventory levels to ensure that a business has the necessary goods and materials to operate efficiently and effectively. In this article, we will discuss the basics of inventory control and management, as well as some best practices for effective inventory management.

Inventory Control and Management Basics

Inventory control and management involves several key components, including inventory tracking, demand forecasting, and inventory optimization. Here are some basic concepts to keep in mind:

Inventory Tracking: This involves the systematic tracking of inventory levels, including the types and quantities of goods and materials on hand. This can be done manually, using spreadsheets or other tracking tools, or through automated inventory management software.

Demand Forecasting: Effective inventory management requires an understanding of demand patterns and trends. Demand forecasting involves using historical sales data, market trends, and other factors to predict future demand for goods and materials.

Inventory Optimization: Once inventory levels and demand patterns have been established, inventory optimization involves setting optimal inventory levels and reorder points to ensure that the business has the necessary goods and materials on hand, without overstocking and wasting resources.

Best Practices for Effective Inventory Management

Effective inventory management requires careful planning, tracking, and optimization. Here are some best practices for effective inventory control and management:

Set Optimal Inventory Levels: To avoid stockouts and overstocking, it's important to set optimal inventory levels based on demand patterns, lead times, and other factors. This involves calculating safety stock levels, reorder points, and economic order quantities to ensure that the business has the necessary goods and materials on hand, without excess inventory.

Use Technology: Automated inventory management software can help streamline the inventory tracking process and provide real-time inventory visibility. This can help businesses stay on top of inventory levels, reduce the risk of stockouts, and optimize inventory levels.

Conduct Regular Audits: Regular inventory audits can help identify discrepancies and inaccuracies in inventory levels, as well as opportunities for improvement. This can involve physical inventory counts, cycle counts, and spot checks to ensure that inventory levels are accurate and up-to-date.

Implement Inventory Controls: To prevent theft, loss, and other types of inventory shrinkage, it's important to implement inventory controls such as security measures, inventory tracking procedures, and access controls.

Use Data Analytics: Data analytics tools can be used to identify trends and patterns in inventory levels, as well as to forecast demand and optimize inventory levels. This can help businesses make more informed inventory management decisions and improve overall efficiency.

Plan for Seasonal Demand: Seasonal demand fluctuations can have a significant impact on inventory levels and demand forecasting. To avoid stockouts and overstocking, it's important to plan for seasonal demand and adjust inventory levels accordingly.

Build Strong Relationships with Suppliers: Effective inventory management requires strong relationships with suppliers, who can provide reliable delivery times, quality products, and competitive pricing. Building strong supplier relationships can help businesses optimize inventory levels, reduce costs, and improve overall efficiency.

Conclusion

Effective inventory control and management is critical to the success of any business, regardless of the industry. By implementing best practices for inventory tracking, demand forecasting, and inventory optimization, businesses can ensure that they have the necessary goods and materials on hand to operate efficiently and effectively. Additionally, by leveraging technology, data analytics, and strong supplier relationships, businesses can further optimize their inventory levels and improve overall efficiency.

Guest satisfaction is a critical factor in the success of any hospitality business. Whether it's a hotel, restaurant, or any other hospitality establishment, the satisfaction of the guests should always be a top priority. In this article, we will discuss the importance of guest satisfaction, how to measure it, and best practices for handling guest complaints.

Importance of Guest Satisfaction

Guest satisfaction is essential for any hospitality business to succeed. Satisfied guests are more likely to return to the establishment, recommend it to others, and leave positive reviews. On the other hand, dissatisfied guests are more likely to leave negative reviews, share their negative experiences with others, and never return. Therefore, guest satisfaction should always be a top priority for any hospitality business.

Measuring Guest Satisfaction

Measuring guest satisfaction is essential for hospitality businesses to understand how well they are meeting their guests' expectations. Here are some common methods of measuring guest satisfaction:

Surveys: Surveys are a popular way of measuring guest satisfaction. These surveys can be conducted in-person, via email, or through an online platform. Surveys typically ask guests about their experience, including their satisfaction with the service, amenities, and overall experience.

Online Reviews: Online reviews on platforms like TripAdvisor, Yelp, and Google Reviews can also provide insights into guest satisfaction. These reviews can be analyzed to identify trends and areas for improvement.

Guest Feedback: Guest feedback can also provide insights into guest satisfaction. This feedback can be gathered through comment cards, feedback forms, or through conversations with guests.

Best Practices for Handling Guest Complaints

Handling guest complaints is a critical part of managing guest satisfaction. Here are some best practices for handling guest complaints:

Listen and Empathize: When a guest complains, it's essential to listen carefully to their concerns and show empathy. Acknowledge their concerns, and take the time to understand their perspective.

Respond Quickly: Responding quickly to guest complaints is essential to prevent the issue from escalating. Address the guest's concerns as soon as possible, and communicate clearly about what steps are being taken to address the issue.

Apologize: Apologizing to guests who have experienced an issue is essential to show that their concerns are being taken seriously. Apologize sincerely, and take responsibility for the issue, even if it wasn't the establishment's fault.

Take Action: Once the issue has been identified, take appropriate action to address it. This may involve offering compensation or making changes to the establishment's policies or procedures to prevent similar issues from happening in the future.

Follow Up: After the issue has been resolved, follow up with the guest to ensure that they are satisfied with the resolution. This can help to restore their confidence in the establishment and prevent similar issues from happening in the future.

Conclusion

Guest satisfaction is critical for the success of any hospitality business. By measuring guest satisfaction through surveys, online reviews, and guest feedback, hospitality businesses can identify areas for improvement and ensure that their guests are happy. Additionally, by handling guest complaints effectively and following best practices, hospitality businesses can prevent issues from escalating and ensure that guests feel heard and valued. Ultimately, prioritizing guest satisfaction can help hospitality businesses to build a loyal customer base and achieve long-term success.

Module 3: Customer Service

In any business, customer service is a critical component of success. In the hospitality industry, customer service can make or break an establishment's reputation. In this module, we will discuss the importance of customer service, how to provide excellent customer service, and how to handle customer complaints.

Importance of Customer Service

Customer service is important for several reasons. First, it can help to build a loyal customer base. When customers receive excellent service, they are more likely to return to the establishment and recommend it to others. Second, it can set an establishment apart from its competitors. In a competitive market, providing excellent customer service can be a way to differentiate an establishment from others. Finally, excellent customer service can improve an establishment's reputation. Positive reviews and word-of-mouth recommendations can lead to increased business and revenue.

Providing Excellent Customer Service

Providing excellent customer service involves several key components. Here are some best practices for providing excellent customer service:

Be Friendly and Engaging: Greet customers with a smile and make eye contact. Use their name if possible and engage in small talk if appropriate. This can help to make customers feel welcome and valued.

Listen Carefully: Listen carefully to customers' concerns and needs. Repeat back what they have said to ensure that you understand their concerns.

Anticipate Needs: Anticipate customers' needs and provide them with what they need before they ask. For example, if a customer is looking for a menu, offer to bring them one before they ask.

Be Knowledgeable: Have a thorough knowledge of the establishment's products and services. This can help to answer customers' questions and provide recommendations.

Be Attentive: Be attentive to customers' needs throughout their visit. Check on them periodically and ask if there is anything else they need.

Handling Customer Complaints

Handling customer complaints effectively is essential to maintaining customer satisfaction. Here are some best practices for handling customer complaints:

Listen: Listen carefully to the customer's complaint. Repeat back what they have said to ensure that you understand their concerns.

Apologize: Apologize for any inconvenience or frustration the customer has experienced. Be sincere in your apology and take responsibility for any mistakes or issues.

Address the Issue: Take appropriate action to address the customer's complaint. This may involve offering a refund, a discount, or making a change to the establishment's policies or procedures.

Follow Up: Follow up with the customer after the issue has been resolved to ensure that they are satisfied with the resolution.

Document the Complaint: Document the complaint in detail, including the customer's name, the date and time of the complaint, and the steps taken to resolve the issue. This can help to identify trends and areas for improvement.

Conclusion

Providing excellent customer service is essential for any hospitality business to succeed. By being friendly and engaging, listening carefully, anticipating needs, being knowledgeable, and being attentive, businesses can provide a positive customer experience. Additionally, handling customer complaints effectively by listening, apologizing, addressing the issue, following up, and documenting the complaint can help to maintain customer satisfaction and prevent issues from escalating. Ultimately, prioritizing customer service can help hospitality businesses to build a loyal customer base, set themselves apart from competitors, and improve their reputation.

Understanding Customer Service in the Hospitality Industry

Customer service is an integral part of any business, and the hospitality industry is no exception. In this industry, customers expect not only a high level of service, but also an exceptional experience that makes them feel valued and cared for. In this article, we will discuss the importance of customer service in the hospitality industry, the key elements of customer service, and how to train staff to provide excellent customer service.

Importance of Customer Service in the Hospitality Industry

In the hospitality industry, customer service plays a crucial role in shaping customers' perceptions and experiences. From the moment a customer walks through the door to the time they check out, they expect to be treated with respect and professionalism. The quality of customer service can have a significant impact on customer loyalty, word-of-mouth referrals, and overall profitability.

Customers in the hospitality industry are not just buying a product or service, but they are also buying an experience. They want to feel welcomed, comfortable, and cared for. They expect staff to anticipate their needs and provide personalized service. In this highly competitive industry, excellent customer service can be a key differentiator that sets an establishment apart from its competitors.

Key Elements of Customer Service in the Hospitality Industry

Providing excellent customer service in the hospitality industry requires attention to several key elements. These include:

Communication: Communication is critical in the hospitality industry. Staff must be able to communicate effectively with customers to understand their needs and provide the appropriate service. Communication also involves active listening, responding to customer feedback, and providing clear and concise information.

Professionalism: In the hospitality industry, staff must maintain a high level of professionalism at all times. This includes dressing appropriately, being punctual, and maintaining a positive attitude.

Attention to Detail: Attention to detail is essential in the hospitality industry. Staff must be able create a positive customer experience that meets and exceeds customers' expectations. Communication, professionalism, attention to detail, empathy, and efficiency are all essential elements of customer service that hospitality staff should be trained to understand and apply in their work. By setting clear expectations, providing comprehensive training, modeling behavior, providing feedback, and recognizing and rewarding excellent service, hospitality businesses can ensure that their staff provides exceptional customer service that leaves a lasting impression on customers. Overall, customer service is not just a part of the hospitality industry, but it is the heart and soul of the industry that keeps customers coming back for more.

Effective communication skills are essential for success in both personal and professional life. Communication skills are not just limited to verbal communication, but also include nonverbal communication, such as body language and facial expressions. Being able to communicate effectively can help build relationships, solve problems, and achieve goals.

There are several key elements of effective communication skills. The first is clarity. When communicating with others, it is important to be clear and concise in your message. This means using simple language and avoiding jargon or technical terms that others may not understand. It also means organizing your thoughts before you speak or write, so that your message is easy to follow.

Another important element of effective communication is active listening. Active listening involves paying attention to what the other person is saying, and responding in a way that shows you understand their perspective. This means avoiding distractions, such as checking your phone or thinking about what you are going to say next. It also means asking questions and summarizing what the other person has said to ensure that you have understood their message.

Body language is also an important aspect of effective communication. Nonverbal cues such as facial expressions, gestures, and posture can convey as much, if not more, information than words. For example, a smile can indicate happiness or friendliness, while a frown can indicate disapproval or unhappiness. Similarly, crossing your arms can indicate defensiveness or closed-mindedness, while open body language can indicate openness and receptiveness.

The tone of voice is another important aspect of effective communication. The tone of voice can convey emotions such as anger, frustration, or happiness. It is important to use an appropriate tone of voice that matches the message you are trying to convey. For example, if you are giving feedback to an employee, it is important to use a calm and constructive tone of voice, rather than a confrontational or aggressive tone.

Effective communication skills can be applied in a variety of settings, from personal relationships to the workplace. In personal relationships, effective communication can help build trust and understanding between partners. This can involve expressing your feelings and needs clearly, and listening actively to your partner's concerns. It can also involve using positive language and avoiding negative language that can cause conflict or hurt feelings.

In the workplace, effective communication skills are essential for success. Effective communication can help build strong relationships with colleagues, managers, and clients. It can also help solve problems and make decisions more efficiently. In the workplace, effective communication can involve giving clear instructions, providing feedback, and listening actively to others' perspectives.

One of the most important aspects of effective communication in the workplace is the ability to communicate with people from diverse backgrounds. This means being aware of cultural differences and adapting your communication style accordingly. For example, in some cultures, direct communication is valued, while in others, indirect communication is preferred. Similarly, in some cultures, maintaining eye contact is seen as a sign of respect, while in others, it is considered rude.

In order to improve your communication skills, there are several strategies that you can use. The first is to practice active listening. This means paying attention to what others are saying and responding in a way that shows you understand their perspective. It can also involve asking questions and clarifying information to ensure that you have understood the message.

Another strategy for improving your communication skills is to practice clarity. This means using simple language and avoiding jargon or technical terms that others may not understand. It also means organizing your thoughts before you speak or write, so that your message is easy to follow.

Body language is another important aspect of effective communication that can be improved through practice. This involves being aware of your own body language and using it to convey positive messages. For example, maintaining eye contact, smiling, and using open body language can all convey openness and receptiveness.

Finally, practicing your communication skills in a variety of settings can also help improve your overall effectiveness. This can involve engaging in conversations with friends or colleagues, giving presentations or speeches, or participating in group discussions or debates.

Another way to improve your communication skills is to seek feedback from others. Asking for feedback from colleagues, friends, or family members can help you identify areas where you can improve, as well as areas where you are already effective. This can involve asking for feedback on specific communication skills, such as active listening or clarity, or more general feedback on your communication style and effectiveness.

It is also important to be aware of potential barriers to effective communication. These can include language barriers, cultural differences, and personal biases or prejudices. Being aware of these barriers can help you take steps to overcome them, such as using simple language or adapting your communication style to better match the cultural norms of the person you are communicating with.

In addition, it is important to be mindful of your own emotions and reactions when communicating with others. This means being aware of your own biases and prejudices, as well as any emotions that may be clouding your judgment or making it difficult to communicate effectively. It can also involve taking steps to manage your own emotions, such as taking a break or deep breath before responding to a challenging message.

Finally, effective communication skills require ongoing practice and development. This means continuing to seek out opportunities to improve your communication skills, such as attending workshops or training sessions, reading books or articles on communication, or seeking out feedback from colleagues or mentors.

In conclusion, effective communication skills are essential for success in both personal and professional life. Key elements of effective communication include clarity, active listening, body language, and tone of voice. Effective communication can help build relationships, solve problems, and achieve goals. Strategies for improving your communication skills include practicing active listening, clarity, and body language, seeking feedback from others, being aware of potential barriers to effective communication, and continuing to practice and develop your skills over time.

Meeting and exceeding customer expectations is critical to the success of any business. In today's highly competitive marketplace, customers have more choices than ever before, and businesses that fail to deliver on their promises are likely to lose customers to competitors. To remain competitive, businesses must focus on understanding and meeting their customers' needs and expectations.

Understanding customer expectations

The first step in meeting and exceeding customer expectations is to understand what those expectations are. This involves listening to customer feedback, conducting market research, and analyzing customer behavior to identify patterns and trends.

One effective way to gather customer feedback is through surveys or focus groups. These tools can provide valuable insights into customer preferences, attitudes, and behaviors, as well as identify areas where improvements can be made.

Market research can also be a valuable tool for understanding customer expectations. This may involve analyzing industry trends, competitor strategies, and customer demographics to identify opportunities and potential areas of improvement.

Analyzing customer behavior can also provide valuable insights into customer expectations. This may involve tracking customer purchases, website activity, or social media interactions to identify patterns and trends.

Meeting customer expectations

Once customer expectations have been identified, the next step is to meet those expectations. This involves delivering on promises, providing high-quality products and services, and providing exceptional customer service.

One key aspect of meeting customer expectations is delivering on promises. This means being transparent and honest about what your business can deliver, and ensuring that you follow through on those promises. For example, if you promise a certain delivery date for a product, it is important to deliver the product on that date, or communicate any delays as soon as possible.

Providing high-quality products and services is another important aspect of meeting customer expectations. This means delivering products or services that meet or exceed customer expectations in terms of quality, value, and performance. This may involve investing in product development or service improvements, or making changes to processes or procedures to improve quality and efficiency.

Providing exceptional customer service is also critical to meeting customer expectations. This means being responsive to customer inquiries and concerns, providing timely and accurate information, and going above and beyond to ensure that customers are satisfied with their experience. This may involve training employees to provide exceptional customer service, or investing in technology or tools that can improve the customer experience.

Exceeding customer expectations

While meeting customer expectations is important, businesses that want to stand out in a crowded marketplace must also strive to exceed those expectations. This involves delivering exceptional experiences that go above and beyond what customers expect.

One effective way to exceed customer expectations is by providing personalized experiences. This means tailoring products or services to meet the unique needs and preferences of individual customers. For example, a clothing retailer might use data analytics to recommend products based on a customer's previous purchases or browsing history.

Providing proactive customer service is another effective way to exceed customer expectations. This means anticipating customer needs and taking action to address them before they become issues. For example, a hotel might offer early check-in or late check-out options to accommodate the needs of travelers with early or late flights.

Offering value-added services or products is also an effective way to exceed customer expectations. This means providing additional products or services that complement or enhance the core offering, such as free shipping, extended warranties, or complementary products. For example, a car dealer might offer free car washes or oil changes to customers who purchase a new vehicle.

Finally, creating emotional connections with customers can help exceed their expectations. This means engaging with customers in a way that resonates with their emotions, such as by telling compelling stories or providing experiences that create positive emotions. For example, a restaurant might create a memorable dining experience by offering live music or a unique ambiance that sets it apart from other restaurants.

Benefits of meeting and exceeding customer expectations

Meeting and exceeding customer expectations can provide a range of benefits for businesses including:

Increased customer loyalty: When businesses consistently meet or exceed customer expectations, customers are more likely to remain loyal and continue to purchase products or services from that business.

Positive word-of-mouth: Satisfied customers are more likely to recommend a business to others, which can help attract new customers and expand the business's customer base.

Improved reputation: A reputation for meeting or exceeding customer expectations can help build trust and credibility with customers, which can in turn lead to increased sales and revenue.

Increased revenue: Meeting and exceeding customer expectations can lead to increased customer retention, repeat business, and referrals, which can all contribute to increased revenue for the business.

Competitive advantage: Businesses that consistently meet or exceed customer expectations are more likely to stand out in a crowded marketplace and gain a competitive advantage over their rivals.

Strategies for meeting and exceeding customer expectations

There are a number of strategies that businesses can use to meet and exceed customer expectations. These include:

Clearly defining and communicating customer expectations: Businesses should be transparent about what customers can expect in terms of products, services, and customer support. This can help manage customer expectations and avoid disappointment.

Investing in product development and service improvements: Businesses that continuously invest in product development and service improvements are more likely to meet or exceed customer expectations in terms of quality, value, and performance.

Providing exceptional customer service: Businesses should prioritize providing exceptional customer service, including being responsive to customer inquiries and concerns, providing timely and accurate information, and going above and beyond to ensure customer satisfaction.

Personalizing the customer experience: By tailoring products or services to meet the unique needs and preferences of individual customers, businesses can create a more personalized experience that exceeds customer expectations.

Offering value-added services or products: Businesses can exceed customer expectations by providing additional products or services that complement or enhance the core offering, such as free shipping, extended warranties, or complementary products.

Creating emotional connections with customers: By engaging with customers in a way that resonates with their emotions, businesses can create a deeper, more meaningful connection with customers that exceeds their expectations.

In conclusion, meeting and exceeding customer expectations is critical to the success of any business. By understanding customer expectations, delivering high-quality products and services, and providing exceptional customer service, businesses can build customer loyalty, improve their reputation, and gain a competitive advantage. By going above and beyond to personalize the customer experience, offer value-added services or products, and create emotional connections with customers, businesses can exceed customer expectations and stand out in a crowded marketplace.

Handling customer complaints is an important part of customer service. When customers are unhappy with a product or service, they are likely to voice their concerns, and businesses need to be prepared to handle these complaints in a professional and effective manner. Effective complaint handling can help turn dissatisfied customers into loyal customers, improve the reputation of the business, and ultimately drive revenue growth. In this article, we will explore the key strategies for handling customer complaints effectively.

Listen to the customer

The first step in handling customer complaints is to listen to the customer. It is important to let the customer express their concerns fully without interrupting or becoming defensive. Listening attentively will show the customer that you are taking their concerns seriously and that you are committed to resolving the issue. It is also important to ask questions to clarify the customer's concerns and to gather all the information necessary to resolve the issue.

Apologize and take responsibility

After listening to the customer, it is important to apologize and take responsibility for any mistakes or issues that have occurred. Even if the issue was not the fault of the business, it is important to acknowledge the customer's feelings and apologize for any inconvenience they may have experienced. Taking responsibility for the issue will help to build trust and credibility with the customer and show that the business is committed to resolving the issue.

Resolve the issue

Once the customer's concerns have been fully understood, it is important to take action to resolve the issue. This may involve offering a refund, providing a replacement product or service, or finding another solution that meets the customer's needs. It is important to work with the customer to find a solution that they are satisfied with, even if it involves some extra effort or cost on the part of the business.

Follow up with the customer

After the issue has been resolved, it is important to follow up with the customer to ensure that they are satisfied with the resolution. This can be done through a phone call, email, or survey. Following up with the customer shows that the business is committed to providing excellent customer service and can help to build a long-term relationship with the customer.

Learn from the experience

Handling customer complaints can be a valuable learning experience for businesses. By analyzing the root causes of customer complaints, businesses can identify areas for improvement and make changes to prevent similar issues from occurring in the future. This can help to improve the quality of the product or service and enhance the overall customer experience.

Train employees on effective complaint handling

Effective complaint handling requires specific skills and training. Businesses should provide employees with the necessary training to handle complaints professionally and effectively. This may include training on active listening, problem-solving, and conflict resolution. Providing employees with the necessary training and support will help to ensure that customer complaints are handled in a consistent and effective manner.

Use technology to streamline complaint handling

Technology can be a valuable tool for handling customer complaints. Customer service software, for example, can help to streamline the complaint handling process by organizing customer information and providing a centralized platform for responding to customer inquiries. Chatbots and other artificial intelligence tools can also help to automate certain aspects of complaint handling, such as responding to common inquiries or routing inquiries to the appropriate department.

In conclusion, handling customer complaints is a critical part of providing excellent customer service. By listening to the customer, apologizing and taking responsibility, resolving the issue, following up, learning from the experience, training employees, and using technology to streamline the process, businesses can effectively handle customer complaints and build long-term relationships with their customers. Effective complaint handling can help to improve the reputation of the business, increase customer loyalty, and drive revenue growth.

As a business owner or customer service representative, dealing with difficult customers can be challenging. Difficult customers can come in all shapes and sizes, and it's important to know how to handle them in a way that is both professional and effective. In this article, we'll discuss some strategies for managing difficult customers and how to turn their negative experiences into positive ones.

Stay calm and professional

When dealing with difficult customers, it's important to remain calm and professional. This can be easier said than done, especially if the customer is angry or rude. However, it's essential to remember that the customer's behavior is not a reflection of you or your business. By remaining calm and professional, you can defuse the situation and prevent it from escalating.

Listen attentively

When dealing with a difficult customer, it's important to listen attentively to their concerns. This will show the customer that you are taking their concerns seriously and that you value their feedback. Listening to the customer will also help you to understand the root cause of their frustration, which can help you to find a solution that meets their needs.

Empathize with the customer

Empathy is an important skill when dealing with difficult customers. By putting yourself in the customer's shoes, you can understand their perspective and show them that you care about their concerns. This can help to defuse the situation and build trust with the customer. When empathizing with the customer, it's important to use language that shows you understand their feelings, such as "I can see how frustrating this situation must be for you."

Apologize and take responsibility

Even if the issue is not the fault of the business, it's important to apologize and take responsibility for the customer's experience. This can help to defuse the situation and show the customer that you are committed to finding a solution that meets their needs. Apologizing can also help to build trust with the customer and prevent them from spreading negative feedback about the business.

Offer a solution

After listening to the customer's concerns and empathizing with their situation, it's important to offer a solution that meets their needs. This may involve providing a refund, replacing a product or service, or finding another solution that the customer is satisfied with. It's important to work with the customer to find a solution that meets their needs, even if it involves extra effort or cost on the part of the business.

Know when to escalate the situation

In some cases, dealing with difficult customers may require escalating the situation to a higher authority. This may involve bringing in a supervisor or manager to help resolve the issue. It's important to know when to escalate the situation and to communicate clearly with the customer about what steps are being taken to resolve the issue.

Set boundaries

While it's important to empathize with the customer and provide solutions to their concerns, it's also important to set boundaries. If the customer is being verbally abusive or threatening, it's important to assert boundaries and let the customer know that their behavior is not acceptable. This can help to prevent the situation from escalating and ensure that the customer's concerns are addressed in a professional and respectful manner.

Follow up with the customer

After the situation has been resolved, it's important to follow up with the customer to ensure that they are satisfied with the solution. This can help to build a long-term relationship with the customer and prevent similar issues from occurring in the future. Following up with the customer also shows that the business is committed to providing excellent customer service and can help to prevent negative feedback from spreading.

In conclusion, managing difficult customers is an essential skill for businesses and customer service representatives. By staying calm and professional, listening attentively, empathizing with the customer, apologizing and taking responsibility, offering a solution, knowing when to escalate the situation, setting boundaries, and following up with the customer, businesses can turn negative experiences into positive ones and build trust with their customers.

It's important to remember that every customer is different and may require a different approach. Some customers may simply need to vent their frustrations, while others may require a more proactive solution. By using these strategies and adapting them to each individual situation, businesses can effectively manage difficult customers and provide excellent customer service.

It's also important to note that difficult customers can sometimes be the result of poor communication or a lack of clarity on the part of the business.

To prevent these situations from occurring, businesses should strive to communicate clearly and effectively with their customers. This may involve providing clear instructions, setting realistic expectations, and keeping the customer informed throughout the process.

In addition, businesses can take proactive steps to prevent difficult customer situations from occurring in the first place. This may involve providing clear policies and procedures, training staff on effective customer service techniques, and using customer feedback to improve products and services.

Finally, businesses should strive to learn from difficult customer situations and use them as an opportunity for growth and improvement. By analyzing customer feedback and identifying areas for improvement, businesses can make changes that will improve the overall customer experience and prevent similar issues from occurring in the future.

In conclusion, managing difficult customers is an essential skill for businesses and customer service representatives. By staying calm and professional, listening attentively, empathizing with the customer, apologizing and taking responsibility, offering a solution, knowing when to escalate the situation, setting boundaries, and following up with the customer, businesses can turn negative experiences into positive ones and build trust with their customers. With effective communication, clear policies and procedures, and a commitment to continuous improvement, businesses can provide excellent customer service and build long-term relationships with their customers.

Building customer loyalty and retention is a crucial aspect of any business. Retaining existing customers is not only more cost-effective than acquiring new ones but also helps to build a strong brand reputation and generate positive word-of-mouth referrals. In this article, we will explore strategies for building customer loyalty and retention.

Provide exceptional customer service

The first step in building customer loyalty is to provide exceptional customer service. This means going above and beyond to meet and exceed customer expectations. Customers are more likely to remain loyal to a business that provides personalized, attentive, and responsive service. This includes being available to answer questions, resolving issues promptly, and following up with customers to ensure their needs have been met.

Build trust and credibility

Building trust and credibility is another important aspect of building customer loyalty. This involves being transparent and honest with customers, providing accurate information, and delivering on promises. Businesses can build trust by being consistent in their actions and providing a high level of quality in their products or services.

Create a loyalty program

A loyalty program can be an effective way to incentivize customers to continue doing business with a company. This can involve offering exclusive discounts, rewards, or special promotions to loyal customers. Loyalty programs can also provide valuable data on customer behavior, preferences, and spending habits, which can be used to improve the overall customer experience.

Offer personalized experiences

Personalization is becoming increasingly important in today's business landscape. Customers expect businesses to know their preferences and provide personalized experiences. This can involve tailoring products or services to meet the unique needs of individual customers, providing personalized recommendations, or sending personalized communications.

Provide ongoing communication

Providing ongoing communication with customers is essential for building loyalty and retention. This includes keeping customers informed of new products, services, and promotions, as well as providing updates on their orders or accounts. Regular communication also helps businesses to stay top-of-mind with customers and reminds them of the value they provide.

Create a positive customer experience

Creating a positive customer experience is critical for building customer loyalty and retention. This involves creating a seamless and enjoyable experience across all touchpoints, from the initial inquiry to the post-purchase follow-up. Businesses can achieve this by focusing on the customer journey and identifying areas for improvement.

Address customer complaints promptly

Addressing customer complaints promptly and effectively is another key aspect of building customer loyalty. This involves listening to the customer's concerns, acknowledging their frustrations, and providing a timely solution. By addressing complaints in a professional and empathetic manner, businesses can turn negative experiences into positive ones and build trust with their customers.

Use customer feedback to improve

Finally, businesses can use customer feedback to continuously improve the customer experience. This involves gathering feedback through surveys, social media, or other channels and using this feedback to identify areas for improvement. By taking action on customer feedback, businesses can demonstrate their commitment to providing exceptional customer service and build loyalty with their customers.

In conclusion, building customer loyalty and retention is essential for any business. By providing exceptional customer service, building trust and credibility, creating a loyalty program, offering personalized experiences, providing ongoing communication, creating a positive customer experience, addressing customer complaints promptly, and using customer feedback to improve, businesses can build long-term relationships with their customers and create a strong brand reputation.

In any business, there will be times when things go wrong and customers are left unsatisfied. Service recovery strategies are the set of actions that businesses take to regain the trust and satisfaction of their customers after a negative experience. Effective service recovery can not only resolve the immediate issue but can also improve customer loyalty and increase repeat business. In this article, we will explore some service recovery strategies that businesses can use to turn a negative experience into a positive one.

Listen to the customer

The first step in effective service recovery is to listen to the customer's concerns. This means giving the customer the opportunity to express their dissatisfaction and ensuring that you understand their perspective. Listening attentively and empathizing with the customer can help to diffuse the situation and demonstrate that you care about their experience.

Apologize and take responsibility

After listening to the customer, it's important to apologize and take responsibility for the issue. This shows the customer that you are taking their concerns seriously and that you are committed to resolving the issue. A sincere apology can go a long way in restoring trust and satisfaction.

Offer a solution

Once you have apologized and taken responsibility, it's time to offer a solution. This may involve offering a refund, replacing the product or service, or providing compensation. It's important to offer a solution that meets the customer's needs and is appropriate for the situation.

Follow up with the customer

Following up with the customer after the issue has been resolved is an important step in effective service recovery. This shows the customer that you value their business and are committed to ensuring their satisfaction. Following up can also provide an opportunity to gather feedback and identify areas for improvement.

Train employees on effective service recovery

Effective service recovery requires the right skills and training. Businesses should ensure that their employees are trained on effective service recovery strategies and have the authority to resolve customer complaints. This can help to prevent negative experiences from escalating and improve customer satisfaction.

Use customer feedback to improve

Service recovery can also provide valuable feedback that can be used to improve the overall customer experience. Businesses should analyze customer feedback and identify areas for improvement. This can involve improving products or services, revising policies and procedures, or providing additional training for employees.

Respond to negative reviews

In today's digital age, negative reviews can have a significant impact on a business's reputation. It's important to respond promptly and professionally to negative reviews, demonstrating that you take customer feedback seriously and are committed to resolving any issues. A well-crafted response can show potential customers that you are responsive to customer concerns and can help to mitigate the impact of negative reviews.

Provide proactive service

Finally, businesses can use proactive service to prevent negative experiences from occurring in the first place. This can involve providing clear instructions and expectations, setting realistic expectations, and keeping the customer informed throughout the process. By providing proactive service, businesses can build trust with their customers and reduce the likelihood of negative experiences.

In conclusion, effective service recovery is essential for any business that wants to maintain customer satisfaction and loyalty. By listening to the customer, apologizing and taking responsibility, offering a solution, following up with the customer, training employees on effective service recovery, using customer feedback to improve, responding to negative reviews, and providing proactive service, businesses can turn negative experiences into positive ones and build long-term relationships with their customers.

Module 4: Front Office Operations

Module 4 of hospitality management courses typically covers front office operations. This module is important because the front office is the face of a hotel or resort, and the quality of the front office operations can significantly impact the guest experience. In this article, we will explore some of the key topics covered in Module 4 of hospitality management courses.

Front office functions

The front office is responsible for a variety of functions, including guest check-in and check-out, room assignments, guest services, and handling guest complaints. Effective front office operations require a high level of organization, communication, and attention to detail. Front office staff must also have strong customer service skills and be able to remain calm and professional under pressure.

Reservations

Reservations are a critical component of front office operations. The reservation process involves taking bookings for rooms, restaurants, and other hotel amenities. Effective reservation management requires accurate record-keeping, timely communication with guests, and efficient use of available resources.

Room inventory management

Room inventory management involves the efficient allocation of available rooms to guests. This requires a thorough understanding of room types, availability, and pricing. Effective room inventory management can help to maximize revenue and improve the guest experience.

Revenue management

Revenue management is a strategy that hotels use to optimize pricing and availability to maximize revenue. This involves analyzing demand patterns, adjusting room rates based on demand, and offering promotions to attract guests. Revenue management is a critical component of front office operations and requires a high level of analytical and strategic thinking.

Guest services

Guest services are an important part of front office operations. This includes providing information about the hotel and its amenities, responding to guest requests, and handling complaints. Effective guest services require strong communication skills, a positive attitude, and a commitment to providing a high level of service.

Front office technology

Technology is increasingly important in front office operations. This includes software for managing reservations and room inventory, as well as tools for communicating with guests and collecting feedback. Front office staff must be proficient in using technology and able to troubleshoot technical issues that may arise.

Security and safety

Security and safety are important considerations in front office operations. This includes ensuring that only authorized guests have access to the hotel and its amenities, as well as monitoring for potential safety hazards. Front office staff must be trained in security and safety protocols and able to respond quickly and effectively in the event of an emergency.

Teamwork and collaboration

Effective front office operations require strong teamwork and collaboration. Front office staff must be able to work together to ensure that guests receive a high level of service. This requires effective communication, a willingness to help each other out, and a commitment to working towards common goals.

In conclusion, front office operations are a critical component of hospitality management courses. Effective front office operations require a high level of organization, communication, and attention to detail. Key topics covered in Module 4 of hospitality management courses include front office functions, reservations, room inventory management, revenue management, guest services, front office technology, security and safety, and teamwork and collaboration. By mastering these topics, hospitality management students can develop the skills and knowledge necessary to succeed in front office operations and provide a high level of service to hotel guests.

The front office is the first point of contact for guests in any hospitality establishment, and it is the responsibility of the front office staff to ensure that guests have a positive experience from the moment they arrive. The role and responsibilities of front office staff are critical to the success of a hotel, resort, or any other hospitality establishment. In this article, we will discuss the key roles and responsibilities of front office staff in detail.

Guest reception and check-in The primary role of front office staff is to welcome guests and facilitate the check-in process. This involves verifying the guest's identity, providing information about the hotel's facilities and services, and ensuring that the guest's preferences are met. Front office staff must also collect payment for the guest's stay and issue room keys. They must be able to communicate effectively with guests and provide a warm and welcoming environment.

Room assignments and inventory management Front office staff are responsible for managing the hotel's room inventory and ensuring that guests are assigned appropriate rooms. This requires an understanding of the hotel's room types and configurations, as well as an awareness of room availability and occupancy levels. Front office staff must be able to balance the needs of guests with the hotel's revenue goals and allocate rooms accordingly.

Reservations management Front office staff are responsible for managing the hotel's reservations system. This includes responding to inquiries about room availability, processing reservations, and updating the hotel's database with guest information. Front office staff must be proficient in using reservation management software and able to provide accurate and timely information to guests.

Guest services Front office staff are responsible for providing a wide range of guest services, including concierge services, transportation arrangements, and providing information about local attractions and events. They must be able to anticipate the needs of guests and provide a high level of personalized service. Front office staff must also be able to respond to guest complaints and resolve issues in a timely and professional manner.

Cash and payment handling Front office staff are responsible for handling cash and processing payments for guest services. This includes processing credit card transactions, issuing receipts, and balancing the cash drawer at the end of each shift. Front office staff must be able to accurately and efficiently process payments and maintain the security of the hotel's cash and payment systems.

Front office administration Front office staff are responsible for a wide range of administrative tasks, including maintaining guest records, preparing reports, and updating hotel databases. They must be proficient in using office software and able to perform data entry and analysis tasks. Front office staff must also be able to maintain accurate and up-to-date records to facilitate efficient hotel operations.

Safety and security Front office staff are responsible for ensuring the safety and security of guests and hotel property. This includes monitoring access to the hotel and ensuring that only authorized guests are allowed on the premises. Front office staff must also be able to respond quickly and effectively to emergency situations and be trained in basic first aid and emergency response procedures.

Teamwork and communication Front office staff must work closely with other hotel staff to ensure the smooth operation of the hotel. This requires effective communication skills and a willingness to collaborate with other departments. Front office staff must also be able to work effectively as part of a team, sharing information and supporting colleagues when necessary.

In conclusion, front office staff play a critical role in the success of any hospitality establishment. They are responsible for a wide range of tasks, including guest reception and check-in, room assignments and inventory management, reservations management, guest services, cash and payment handling, front office administration, safety and security, and teamwork and communication. By mastering these roles and responsibilities, front office staff can provide a high level of service to guests and contribute to the overall success of the hotel.

Front office management is an essential aspect of any hospitality establishment, and it involves a wide range of procedures that are critical to the efficient and effective operation of the front office. In this article, we will discuss the key front office management and procedures that hotel managers must consider.

Organizational structure

The organizational structure of a hotel's front office will depend on the size and complexity of the establishment. In general, however, the front office will consist of several departments, including reception, reservations, guest services, and cash handling. The organizational structure should be designed to facilitate efficient communication and coordination between departments and to ensure that each department is staffed appropriately.

Staff recruitment and training

Recruiting and training front office staff is critical to the success of any hospitality establishment. Front office staff should be recruited based on their knowledge, skills, and experience in the hospitality industry. The training program should be designed to provide staff with the necessary knowledge and skills to perform their roles effectively. This includes training on communication skills, customer service, cash handling, and reservations management.

Front office procedures

Front office procedures are essential to the smooth operation of the hotel. These procedures include the check-in and check-out process, room allocation and inventory management, reservations management, and cash handling procedures. The procedures should be designed to ensure that guests are served efficiently and that the hotel's financial transactions are accurate and secure.

Guest communication and feedback

Effective communication with guests is critical to the success of the front office. Front office staff must be able to communicate effectively with guests and respond to their needs and requests promptly. This includes providing accurate and timely information about the hotel's facilities and services and resolving complaints and issues in a professional manner. The hotel should also have a feedback system in place to gather feedback from guests and to identify areas for improvement.

Technology and software

Technology plays a crucial role in front office management, and the use of the right software and hardware can significantly improve efficiency and effectiveness. Front office staff should be trained in the use of technology such as reservation management software, property management systems, and point-of-sale systems. The software should be updated regularly to ensure that it is functioning correctly and to incorporate new features and functionality.

Security and safety

Security and safety are critical concerns for any hospitality establishment. Front office staff should be trained in emergency response procedures and first aid. The hotel should also have security measures in place, such as access control systems, CCTV, and fire safety systems, to ensure the safety and security of guests and staff.

Performance metrics and analysis

The performance of the front office can be measured and analyzed using a range of metrics, including occupancy rates, revenue per available room, and guest satisfaction scores. These metrics can be used to identify areas for improvement and to track the effectiveness of front office management procedures. Regular performance analysis should be conducted, and staff should be trained in data analysis to ensure that the hotel's performance is optimized.

Continuous improvement

Continuous improvement is critical to the success of any hospitality establishment. The front office should be regularly reviewed and updated to ensure that it is operating effectively and efficiently. This includes updating procedures, training staff, and implementing new technology and software. Regular customer feedback should be collected and analyzed, and improvements should be made based on this feedback.

In conclusion, front office management and procedures are critical to the efficient and effective operation of any hospitality establishment. The organizational structure should be designed to facilitate efficient communication and coordination between departments, and staff should be recruited and trained based on their knowledge and skills. Front office procedures should be designed to ensure that guests are served efficiently, and technology and software should be used to improve efficiency and effectiveness. Security and safety are critical concerns, and performance metrics should be used to identify areas for improvement. Continuous improvement should be prioritized, and regular reviews and updates should be conducted to ensure that the front office is operating effectively and efficiently. By implementing these key front office management and procedures, hospitality establishments can provide a high level of service to guests and ensure the smooth operation of their front office.

Reservation management

Reservation management is a critical aspect of front office operations, and it involves managing room availability, rates, and customer bookings. The reservation system should be user-friendly and efficient to ensure that guests can easily book their stay at the hotel. Staff should also be trained in reservation management procedures to ensure that reservations are managed accurately and efficiently.

Check-in and check-out procedures

Check-in and check-out procedures are among the most critical front office procedures, and they must be managed efficiently to ensure that guests have a positive experience. The check-in process should be streamlined, and guests should be greeted warmly and provided with all the information they need for their stay. The check-out process should also be efficient, and guests should be thanked for their stay and offered assistance with their luggage and transportation.

Guest services

Guest services are essential to ensuring that guests have a positive experience at the hotel. Front office staff should be trained to provide exceptional customer service and to respond to guest requests and needs promptly. Guest services should include providing information about local attractions and activities, arranging transportation, and ensuring that guests have everything they need for their stay.

Cash handling procedures

Cash handling procedures are critical to the financial success of any hospitality establishment. The front office should have strict cash handling procedures in place to ensure that financial transactions are accurate and secure. Staff should be trained in cash handling procedures, and the hotel should have safeguards in place, such as CCTV cameras, to prevent theft and fraud.

Inventory management

Inventory management is essential to the smooth operation of the front office. The hotel should have a system in place to manage room inventory, including room availability, room types, and rates. The front office should also manage inventory for other hotel services, such as food and beverage and guest amenities. This ensures that the hotel has the necessary resources to serve guests efficiently and effectively.

Communication with other departments

Effective communication with other hotel departments is essential to the smooth operation of the front office. The front office should communicate regularly with housekeeping, maintenance, and food and beverage departments to ensure that guest needs are met promptly. This includes coordinating room cleaning and maintenance, providing timely room service, and ensuring that food and beverage orders are delivered promptly.

In conclusion, front office management and procedures are critical to the success of any hospitality establishment. By implementing effective organizational structures, staff recruitment and training programs, efficient front office procedures, and effective communication with guests and other hotel departments, hospitality establishments can provide a high level of service to guests and ensure the smooth operation of their front office. This, in turn, can lead to increased guest satisfaction, improved financial performance, and a positive reputation in the hospitality industry.

Reservation systems and procedures are critical to the success of any hospitality establishment. A reservation system is an automated system that allows guests to book their stay at a hotel, resort, or other accommodation facility. It enables hotels to manage room availability, room rates, and customer bookings efficiently. Effective reservation systems and procedures ensure that the hotel can maximize occupancy rates, improve guest satisfaction, and manage its finances effectively.

Types of Reservation Systems

There are several types of reservation systems available for hotels and other hospitality establishments. These include:

a) Central Reservation System (CRS)

A central reservation system is a software application that enables hotels to manage their room inventory and rates across multiple distribution channels. The CRS integrates with different online travel agencies (OTAs), global distribution systems (GDS), and other third-party platforms, enabling hotels to manage their bookings and rates across different channels from a central platform.

b) Property Management System (PMS)

A property management system is a software application that enables hotels to manage their operations, including room inventory, guest information, and financial transactions. The PMS is a core system that integrates with other hotel systems, including the reservation system, to provide a centralized management platform.

c) Channel Manager

A channel manager is a software application that enables hotels to manage their distribution channels, including OTAs, GDS, and other third-party platforms. The channel manager allows hotels to manage their rates and inventory across different channels from a single platform.

Reservation Procedures

Effective reservation procedures are essential to the success of any hospitality establishment. Reservation procedures should be designed to ensure that guests have a positive experience when making their booking, and that hotel staff can manage bookings efficiently. Here are some essential reservation procedures:

a) Availability Check

Availability check is the first step in the reservation process. It involves checking the hotel's room availability for the dates requested by the guest. The front office staff can check availability through the hotel's reservation system or PMS. If the hotel is fully booked, staff should suggest alternative dates or recommend another hotel in the area.

b) Reservation Request

Once the availability check is complete, the guest can make a reservation request. The request can be made in person, via telephone, or online through the hotel's website or third-party platforms. The guest should provide their personal information, including name, contact details, and payment details.

c) Reservation Confirmation

Once the reservation request is received, the hotel should send a confirmation to the guest. The confirmation should include the reservation details, including room type, rate, check-in, and check-out dates, and payment details. The confirmation should also include the hotel's cancellation policy.

d) Payment and Deposit

Hotels may require guests to pay a deposit or prepayment to secure their reservation. The payment can be made online, via bank transfer, or through the hotel's payment gateway. The hotel should have a secure payment system to ensure that guests' financial information is protected.

e) Cancellation and Modification

Hotels should have a clear cancellation and modification policy to ensure that guests are aware of the terms and conditions. The policy should include the cancellation deadline, the refund policy, and any fees associated with cancellation or modification. Hotels should also provide guests with the option to modify or cancel their reservation online or through the hotel's reservation system.

Benefits of Effective Reservation Systems and Procedures

Effective reservation systems and procedures provide several benefits to hotels and guests. These include:

a) Improved Guest Satisfaction

Effective reservation systems and procedures ensure that guests can book their stay easily and quickly. Guests can check availability, rates, and room types before making a reservation, ensuring that their needs are met. This leads to improved guest satisfaction and a positive reputation for the hotel.

b) Increased Efficiency and Revenue

Effective reservation systems and procedures enable hotels to manage their operations more efficiently. Hotels can manage their room inventory, rates, and distribution channels from a centralized platform, reducing manual errors and improving accuracy. This leads to increased revenue and profitability for the hotel.

c) Better Communication and Coordination Effective reservation systems and procedures enable better communication and coordination between different hotel departments, including the front office, housekeeping, and finance. This ensures that staff can work together seamlessly to provide a positive guest experience.

d) Enhanced Data Management Reservation systems and procedures enable hotels to collect and manage guest data effectively. Hotels can use this data to analyze guest preferences and behavior, and tailor their services accordingly. This leads to improved guest satisfaction and loyalty.

Challenges and Solutions Despite the benefits of effective reservation systems and procedures, there are some challenges that hotels may face. These include:

a) Technical Issues Reservation systems may encounter technical issues, leading to downtime and lost bookings. To mitigate this risk, hotels should invest in reliable and secure reservation systems and backup solutions.

b) Channel Management Managing multiple distribution channels can be challenging, as rates and inventory may differ across channels. Hotels can overcome this challenge by investing in a channel manager that integrates with their reservation system and other hotel systems.

c) Overbooking Overbooking can occur when hotels accept more reservations than their room inventory. This can lead to guest dissatisfaction and lost revenue. To avoid overbooking, hotels should implement a real-time inventory management system that updates availability across all channels.

d) Fraud and Security Reservation systems may be vulnerable to fraud and security breaches. Hotels should implement robust security measures, including secure payment gateways and data encryption, to protect guest information.

Conclusion Effective reservation systems and procedures are essential to the success of any hospitality establishment. They enable hotels to manage their operations efficiently, improve guest satisfaction, and increase revenue. To achieve these benefits, hotels should invest in reliable and secure reservation systems, implement clear reservation procedures, and overcome the challenges associated with reservation management. By doing so, hotels can provide a positive guest experience and achieve long-term success in the competitive hospitality industry.

Check-in and check-out procedures are critical components of front office operations in the hospitality industry. These procedures are vital in ensuring that guests have a seamless experience when arriving and departing from a hotel. In this essay, we will discuss the role and importance of check-in and check-out procedures, as well as the best practices for executing these procedures efficiently.

Role and Importance of Check-In Procedures Check-in procedures refer to the process of welcoming guests to a hotel and ensuring that they have a smooth and hassle-free arrival experience. The check-in process starts with the guest's arrival at the hotel, and it typically involves verifying the guest's identity, registering them, assigning a room, and providing them with necessary information about the hotel and its services.

The importance of check-in procedures cannot be overstated. They are the first point of contact between guests and the hotel, and they set the tone for the rest of the guest's stay. A well-executed check-in process can make guests feel valued and welcome, while a poor check-in experience can lead to frustration and dissatisfaction.

Best Practices for Check-In Procedures To ensure a smooth and efficient check-in process, hotels should follow these best practices:

a) Greet Guests Warmly and Professionally The first impression is crucial, so it's essential to greet guests warmly and professionally. A friendly smile and a sincere greeting can go a long way in making guests feel welcome.

b) Verify Guest Identity It's important to verify the guest's identity by checking their identification documents, such as a passport or driver's license. This ensures that the hotel is complying with legal requirements and reduces the risk of fraud.

c) Collect Guest Information Hotels should collect essential guest information, including their name, contact details, and payment information. This information should be recorded accurately to avoid errors and misunderstandings later on.

d) Provide Information About the Hotel and its Services Hotels should provide guests with necessary information about the hotel and its services. This may include information about dining options, recreational facilities, and nearby attractions. Providing this information proactively can help guests plan their stay more effectively.

e) Assign Room and Provide Room Keys After verifying guest identity and collecting their information, hotels should assign a room and provide room keys. It's important to ensure that the room is clean and ready for the guest's arrival.

f) Provide Assistance with Luggage Hotels should offer assistance with luggage to guests, particularly those with heavy or bulky bags. This service can make guests feel valued and appreciated.

Role and Importance of Check-Out Procedures Check-out procedures refer to the process of a guest departing from a hotel. The check-out process typically involves settling any outstanding charges, returning room keys, and providing guests with any necessary information about their stay.

The importance of check-out procedures is twofold. Firstly, they allow hotels to settle any outstanding charges with guests, ensuring that the hotel is paid for the services provided. Secondly, they provide an opportunity for hotels to gather feedback from guests and identify areas for improvement.

Best Practices for Check-Out Procedures To ensure a smooth and efficient check-out process, hotels should follow these best practices:

a) Anticipate Guest Needs Hotels should anticipate guest needs and offer assistance with any luggage or transportation arrangements. This service can make guests feel valued and appreciated, and it can lead to positive reviews and repeat business.

b) Settle Any Outstanding Charges Hotels should settle any outstanding charges with guests before they depart. This may include room charges, restaurant bills, and any additional services provided during the guest's stay.

c) Provide a Receipt Hotels should provide guests with a receipt that outlines the charges incurred during their stay. This helps guests to understand their bill and provides a record of the transaction.

d) Return Room Keys Hotels should ask guests to return room keys when they check out. This helps to ensure that the keys are not lost or stolen, and it allows the hotel to prepare the room for the next guest.

e) Request Feedback from Guests Hotels should request feedback from guests during the check-out process. This provides an opportunity for hotels to identify areas for improvement and address any issues that may have arisen during the guest's stay.

Conclusion In conclusion, check-in and check-out procedures are essential components of front office operations in the hospitality industry. A well-executed check-in process can make guests feel welcome and valued, while a smooth check-out process can leave guests with a positive impression of the hotel. To ensure that these procedures are carried out efficiently, hotels should follow best practices, including greeting guests warmly, verifying guest identity, collecting guest information, providing information about the hotel and its services, assigning a room, providing room keys, settling any outstanding charges, requesting feedback, and returning room keys. By following these best practices, hotels can provide guests with a seamless and memorable experience, leading to positive reviews, repeat business, and a positive reputation in the hospitality industry.

Guest billing and payment methods are crucial aspects of the hospitality industry. It is essential for hotels to have efficient and accurate billing systems to ensure that guests are charged correctly for the services they have used during their stay. Additionally, providing guests with a variety of payment options can enhance their experience and increase customer satisfaction. In this paper, we will discuss the importance of guest billing and payment methods in the hospitality industry, the different billing methods used in hotels, and the various payment methods available to guests.

Importance of Guest Billing and Payment Methods

Guest billing and payment methods are important for several reasons. Firstly, they ensure that guests are charged correctly for the services they have used during their stay. This helps to avoid any confusion or disputes that may arise over billing discrepancies. Secondly, efficient billing systems can help hotels to streamline their operations and reduce administrative tasks. This can save time and resources, allowing staff to focus on providing high-quality service to guests. Thirdly, providing guests with a variety of payment options can enhance their experience and increase customer satisfaction. By offering convenient payment methods, hotels can make it easier for guests to pay for their stay, improving their overall experience and increasing the likelihood of repeat business.

Billing Methods in Hotels

Hotels use a variety of billing methods to charge guests for their services. These methods include:

Room Charge The room charge method is the most common billing method used in hotels. This method involves charging guests for their room and any additional services they have used during their stay. Guests are usually required to provide a credit card or cash deposit when they check-in to cover any charges they may incur during their stay.

Direct Billing Direct billing is a method used for corporate or group bookings. With this method, the hotel invoices the company or organization directly for the services used by its employees or members. The company or organization then pays the hotel directly, rather than having individual guests pay for their services.

Split Billing Split billing is a method used when different guests sharing a room have different billing preferences. With this method, the hotel charges each guest separately for the services they have used during their stay.

Package Billing Package billing is a method used for guests who have booked a package deal. This method involves charging guests a flat fee for a pre-determined set of services, such as accommodation, meals, and activities.

Payment Methods for Guests

Hotels offer a variety of payment methods to guests. These methods include:

Credit Card Credit cards are the most commonly accepted payment method in the hospitality industry. Guests can use their credit card to pay for their room and any additional services they have used during their stay. Most hotels accept major credit cards, such as Visa, Mastercard, and American Express.

Debit Card Debit cards are also a common payment method in the hospitality industry. Guests can use their debit card to pay for their room and any additional services they have used during their stay. However, it is important to note that some hotels may place a hold on the guest's account to cover any potential charges they may incur during their stay.

Cash Cash is another payment method that is accepted by most hotels. Guests can pay for their room and any additional services they have used during their stay with cash. However, it is important to note that some hotels may require a cash deposit at check-in to cover any potential charges.

Electronic Payment Electronic payment methods, such as PayPal and mobile payment apps, are becoming increasingly popular in the hospitality industry. These methods allow guests to pay for their room and any additional services they have used during their stay using their mobile device or computer.

Traveler's Checks Although traveler's checks are not as commonly used as they once were, some hotels still accept them as a form of payment. Traveler's checks provide a secure way for guests to pay for their services without carrying large amounts of cash.

Gift Cards Many hotels also offer gift cards that guests can use to pay for their stay or other services. Gift cards can be a great option for guests who want to give the gift of travel or for companies looking to provide incentives to their employees.

Guest Billing Procedures

The guest billing process begins when the guest checks-in to the hotel. During the check-in process, the guest provides a method of payment, such as a credit card, and may also be required to provide a cash deposit. The front desk staff then creates a guest folio, which is a record of all the charges incurred by the guest during their stay.

Throughout the guest's stay, any additional charges, such as room service or spa treatments, are added to the guest folio. At check-out, the guest is presented with a final bill, which includes all the charges incurred during their stay. The guest can then review the bill and pay using their preferred method of payment.

It is important for hotels to have efficient billing systems and procedures in place to ensure that guests are charged correctly and that the billing process is as smooth and hassle-free as possible. This includes having staff who are trained in billing procedures, using technology to automate the billing process, and providing guests with clear and detailed bills.

Guest Payment Procedures

Hotels also have procedures in place to ensure that guest payments are processed correctly and securely. This includes using secure payment processing systems, such as point-of-sale terminals and online payment gateways, to process credit card payments. It is also important for hotels to adhere to PCI-DSS (Payment Card Industry Data Security Standard) guidelines to ensure the security of guest payment information.

In addition, hotels may have policies in place for handling payment disputes and chargebacks. Chargebacks occur when a guest disputes a charge on their credit card statement and the hotel is required to provide evidence to support the charge. Hotels should have procedures in place for handling chargebacks and resolving payment disputes to ensure that guests are charged correctly and fairly.

In conclusion, guest billing and payment methods are essential aspects of the hospitality industry. Efficient billing systems and a variety of payment options can enhance the guest experience and increase customer satisfaction. Hotels use a variety of billing methods, including room charge, direct billing, split billing, and package billing, and offer a variety of payment options, including credit card, debit card, cash, electronic payment, traveler's checks, and gift cards.

Effective billing and payment procedures require trained staff, efficient technology, and adherence to security standards and policies. By providing efficient and accurate billing systems and a variety of payment options, hotels can ensure that guests have a seamless and enjoyable experience, increasing the likelihood of repeat business and positive reviews.

Safety and security are critical components of the hospitality industry. Guests have a reasonable expectation of feeling safe and secure while staying in a hotel or resort. Therefore, it is essential for hotels to have well-developed safety and security procedures in place to ensure the safety and well-being of guests, employees, and the property.

Safety Procedures

Safety procedures in hotels may include the following:

Fire Safety

Hotels must adhere to strict fire safety regulations to ensure that guests are safe in case of a fire. This includes having fire alarms, smoke detectors, and sprinkler systems in place, as well as having a fire evacuation plan that is clearly communicated to guests and staff.

Emergency Procedures

Hotels must have procedures in place for emergency situations such as medical emergencies, natural disasters, and other crises. This includes having first aid kits, defibrillators, and emergency phone numbers readily available, as well as training staff on emergency procedures.

Pool Safety

If the hotel has a pool, safety procedures should be in place to ensure that guests are safe while swimming. This includes having lifeguards on duty, providing life jackets for children, and clearly posting pool rules and warnings.

Food Safety

Hotels must also adhere to strict food safety regulations to ensure that guests do not become sick from consuming contaminated food or drinks. This includes training staff in food handling and preparation, regularly inspecting the kitchen and food storage areas, and properly storing and labeling food.

Security Procedures

Security procedures in hotels may include the following:

Access Control

Hotels should have access control procedures in place to ensure that only authorized guests and staff have access to the hotel and guest rooms. This includes using key cards or other security measures to prevent unauthorized access.

Surveillance

Hotels may use surveillance cameras in public areas, such as the lobby and parking lot, to monitor activity and deter criminal behavior. However, it is important to balance guest privacy with security concerns.

Staff Training

Hotel staff should be trained in security procedures, such as identifying and reporting suspicious behavior, handling security incidents, and responding to emergencies.

Background Checks

Hotels should conduct background checks on all employees to ensure that they do not have a criminal history or other red flags that could compromise the safety and security of guests.

Cybersecurity

Hotels must also take steps to protect guests' personal and financial information from cyber attacks. This includes using secure networks and payment systems, encrypting sensitive data, and training staff on cybersecurity best practices.

Conclusion

In conclusion, safety and security procedures are critical to the success of the hospitality industry. Hotels must take steps to ensure the safety and well-being of guests, employees, and the property. Safety procedures may include fire safety, emergency procedures, pool safety, and food safety. Security procedures may include access control, surveillance, staff training, background checks, and cybersecurity.

Effective safety and security procedures require regular training and updates, as well as a commitment to guest safety and well-being. By investing in safety and security measures, hotels can enhance the guest experience and build trust and loyalty among guests, leading to increased business and positive reviews.

Revenue management and sales techniques are essential components of the hospitality industry, particularly in the hotel and resort sector. These techniques help hotels to maximize their revenue and profitability by optimizing occupancy rates and room rates, as well as increasing sales of ancillary services and products.

Revenue Management

Revenue management is the process of optimizing revenue and profitability through the strategic pricing and distribution of hotel inventory. The goal is to maximize revenue by selling the right room, to the right customer, at the right time, for the right price. Revenue management techniques may include:

Demand forecasting - predicting future demand for hotel rooms and adjusting room rates accordingly.

Inventory management - managing the availability of different room types and rates to optimize revenue.

Dynamic pricing - adjusting room rates in real-time based on demand, availability, and other factors.

Channel management - managing the distribution channels through which hotel rooms are sold, such as online travel agencies (OTAs), direct booking channels, and corporate travel agencies.

Yield management - maximizing revenue by selling rooms at the highest possible price without sacrificing occupancy rates.

Sales Techniques

In addition to revenue management, hotels can increase their sales and revenue through effective sales techniques. Sales techniques may include:

Upselling - offering guests additional services or products to enhance their experience, such as room upgrades, spa treatments, or restaurant reservations.

Cross-selling - offering guests additional products or services that complement their current purchase, such as offering a discount on a spa treatment when booking a room.

Package deals - bundling room rates with other products or services to offer a discounted rate and increase sales.

Loyalty programs - offering incentives and rewards to loyal customers to encourage repeat business and increase revenue.

Sales training - training staff on effective sales techniques and customer service skills to increase revenue and build customer loyalty.

Conclusion

Revenue management and sales techniques are critical to the success of hotels and resorts in the hospitality industry. By optimizing revenue through strategic pricing and distribution, hotels can increase profitability and enhance the guest experience. Effective sales techniques can also increase revenue and build customer loyalty by offering additional services, products, and incentives.

To be successful in revenue management and sales, hotels must stay informed on industry trends and constantly adapt their strategies to meet changing market conditions. By investing in revenue management and sales training and technology, hotels can maximize their revenue and position themselves for long-term success in the competitive hospitality industry.

Assessment Model for Module 1: Food Safety and Hygiene

Part A: Multiple Choice Questions (20 points)

Instructions: Choose the best answer for each question.

What is the main purpose of food safety and hygiene?

a) To ensure food tastes good

b) To prevent foodborne illness

c) To increase profits

d) To improve food quality

Which of the following is NOT a food hazard?

a) Physical hazards

b) Chemical hazards

c) Biological hazards

d) Atmospheric hazards

What does HACCP stand for?

a) Hazard Analysis and Critical Control Points

b) Hazardous Allergens in Cooking and Culinary Practices

c) Health and Cooking Control Procedures

d) Healthy and Clean Cooking Practices

What is the purpose of food safety audits and inspections?

a) To ensure compliance with food safety regulations

b) To improve the taste of the food

c) To reduce costs

d) To increase profits

What is the recommended temperature for storing frozen food?

a) Below -18°C

b) Between -10°C and -5°C

c) Between 0°C and 4°C

d) Above 4°C

Part B: Short Answer Questions (30 points)

Instructions: Answer the following questions in one or two sentences.

What are the three types of food hazards?

What is the purpose of personal hygiene in food handling practices?

What is the difference between cleaning and sanitizing?

What is the purpose of HACCP?

What are the steps involved in a food safety audit?

Part C: Essay Question (50 points)

Instructions: Answer the following question in 500 words.

Explain the importance of food safety legislation and regulations in the hospitality industry. Discuss the consequences of not complying with food safety regulations and the impact it can have on both customers and the business.

Assessment Model for Module 2: Hospitality and Hotel Housekeeping

Part A: Multiple Choice Questions (20 points)

Instructions: Choose the best answer for each question.

What is the main purpose of housekeeping in the hospitality industry?

a) To make rooms look nice

b) To increase profits

c) To maintain a clean and safe environment

d) To reduce costs

What are some common cleaning methods used in housekeeping?

a) Vacuuming and sweeping

b) Dusting and wiping

c) Mopping and scrubbing

d) All of the above

What is the purpose of inventory control in housekeeping?

a) To keep track of supplies and equipment

b) To increase profits

c) To reduce costs

d) To improve guest satisfaction

What is the importance of laundry management in housekeeping?

a) To keep guests happy

b) To ensure clean linens and towels are available

c) To reduce costs

d) To increase profits

How should guest complaints be handled in housekeeping?

a) Ignored

b) Acknowledged and addressed immediately

c) Addressed at the end of the day

d) Addressed at the end of the week

Part B: Short Answer Questions (30 points)

Instructions: Answer the following questions in one or two sentences.

What are some common housekeeping supplies and equipment?
What are the steps involved in room preparation and servicing?
What is the purpose of inventory control in housekeeping?
What is the importance of guest satisfaction in housekeeping?
How can housekeeping contribute to the overall guest experience?

Part C: Essay Question (50 points)

Instructions: Answer the following question in 500 words.

Explain the importance of housekeeping in the hospitality industry.

Module 2: Hospitality and Hotel Housekeeping

Multiple-choice questions

a. What is the purpose of housekeeping in a hotel?

i. To keep guests occupied

ii. To keep the hotel looking clean and tidy

iii. To serve food and drinks

iv. To provide entertainment for guests

b. What are the three main types of cleaning?

i. Dusting, vacuuming, and sweeping

ii. Sanitizing, disinfecting, and cleaning

iii. Mopping, scrubbing, and wiping

iv. Washing, drying, and folding

c. What is the purpose of an inventory control system in a hotel?

i. To keep track of guest bookings

ii. To monitor employee attendance

iii. To manage hotel expenses

iv. To track the use of housekeeping supplies and equipment

Essay questions

a. Describe the steps involved in preparing a hotel room for a guest's arrival.

b. Explain the importance of laundry management in a hotel.

c. Discuss effective strategies for managing guest satisfaction and handling complaints.

Module 3: Customer Service

Multiple-choice questions

a. What is the most important element of effective customer service?

i. Friendly staff

ii. A well-designed website

iii. Prompt response to customer inquiries

iv. Understanding and meeting customer needs

b. What is the best way to handle a customer complaint?

i. Ignore the complaint and hope the customer goes away

ii. Argue with the customer and prove them wrong

iii. Listen to the customer, acknowledge their concerns, and offer a solution

iv. Blame the problem on another department or employee

c. What is the key to building customer loyalty?

i. Offering discounts and promotions

ii. Providing exceptional customer service

iii. Adapting to customer preferences

iv. Providing free amenities and upgrades

Essay questions

a. Discuss the importance of effective communication skills in the hospitality industry.

b. Explain the difference between meeting and exceeding customer expectations, and provide examples of each.

c. Describe the steps involved in implementing a service recovery strategy.

Module 4: Front Office Operations

Multiple-choice questions

a. What is the role of the front office staff in a hotel?

i. To provide room service

ii. To manage the hotel's finances

iii. To check guests in and out of the hotel

iv. To perform maintenance tasks

b. What is a reservation system in a hotel?

i. A system for booking guest rooms and other hotel services

ii. A system for managing employee schedules

iii. A system for tracking hotel expenses

iv. A system for ordering supplies and equipment

c. What is the purpose of a safety and security procedure in a hotel?

i. To keep guests entertained and engaged

ii. To prevent accidents and injuries

iii. To reduce hotel expenses

iv. To monitor employee performance

Essay questions

a. Describe the front office management procedures in a hotel, including the roles and responsibilities of front office staff.

b. Discuss the importance of revenue management and sales techniques in the hospitality industry.

c. Explain the process of guest billing and payment methods in a hotel.

Module 3: Customer Service

Multiple choice questions:

a. Which of the following is NOT a customer service skill?

i. Active listening

ii. Time management

iii. Empathy

iv. Patience

b. Which of the following is a method of exceeding customer expectations?

i. Underpromising and overdelivering

ii. Ignoring customer complaints

iii. Offering discounts to customers who complain

iv. Providing mediocre service

c. Which of the following is NOT an effective communication skill?

i. Nonverbal communication

ii. Active listening

iii. Interrupting the speaker

iv. Tone of voice

Short answer questions:

a. Explain the importance of meeting and exceeding customer expectations in the hospitality industry.

b. Describe a time when you had to handle a customer complaint. How did you resolve the issue?

c. Explain how building customer loyalty and retention benefits a hospitality business.

Essay question:

Describe a service recovery strategy that a hospitality business could use to resolve a customer complaint. Provide specific details about the strategy and explain how it could help the business retain the customer's loyalty.

Module 4: Front Office Operations

Multiple choice questions:

a. Which of the following is NOT a responsibility of front office staff?

i. Answering phone calls

ii. Handling guest complaints

iii. Cleaning guest rooms

iv. Checking guests in and out

b. What is the purpose of a reservation system?

i. To ensure that rooms are always available

ii. To allow guests to book rooms in advance

iii. To control the rate of occupancy

iv. To allow staff to know when guests are arriving

c. Which of the following is a common method of payment for guest bills?

i. Cash

ii. Credit card

iii. Cheque

iv. All of the above

Short answer questions:

a. Describe the check-in and check-out procedures for a hotel.

b. Explain the importance of guest billing and payment methods in a hospitality business.

c. Describe the safety and security procedures that front office staff should follow.

Essay question:

Describe the revenue management and sales techniques that a hospitality business could use to increase its revenue. Provide specific examples and explain how they could be implemented in the business.

Question 7:

You are working in a hotel as a housekeeping supervisor. The hotel has received several complaints from guests about their rooms not being properly cleaned and prepared. The general manager has asked you to investigate the matter and report back with recommendations to improve the quality of housekeeping services.

a. What steps would you take to investigate the complaints? b. What are some possible causes of the issue?

c. What recommendations would you make to improve the quality of housekeeping services?

Question 8:

You are working in a front office of a hotel and a guest has just checked in. The guest informs you that they have a severe allergy to peanuts and cannot be exposed to them in any way.

a. What steps would you take to ensure the guest's safety and comfort during their stay? b. What measures can be taken to prevent similar incidents from happening in the future?

Question 9:

You are the manager of a restaurant and have noticed a decrease in customer satisfaction scores. Upon further investigation, you have discovered that the wait staff is not providing the level of service that customers expect.

a. What steps would you take to improve the level of service provided by the wait staff? b. How would you measure the success of your efforts to improve customer satisfaction?

Question 10:

You are working in the front office of a hotel and a guest has just informed you that they need to check out earlier than expected due to a family emergency. The guest was scheduled to stay for two more nights.

a. What steps would you take to handle the guest's request for an early checkout? b. How would you ensure that the guest is satisfied with the resolution of their request?

Printed in Great Britain
by Amazon